To Father Ge.♡ W9-CNF-377
who loves the B
and Fr. B so much

Emile Brière

Immaculate Conception of Our Lady
December 8, 1988

KATIA

A Personal Vision of Catherine de Hueck Doherty

By
Emile Briere
Priest of Madonna House

Éditions Paulines

Phototypesetting: *Les Éditions Paulines*

Cover: *Tony Graf*

Imprimatur: Msgr. Jean-Marie Fortier
Archbishop of Sherbrooke
January 25, 1988

ISBN 2-89039-159-0

Legal deposit — 4th quarter 1988
Bibliothèque nationale du Québec
National Library of Canada

© 1988 Les Éditions Paulines
250, boul. St-François Nord
Sherbrooke, QC, J1E 2B9

Dedication
to Christ who is the Way
through Mary who is the Gate

CONTENTS

INTRODUCTION

Tumbleweed, the first biography of Catherine de Hueck Doherty, was written 40 years ago by her husband, Eddie Doherty. Her former spiritual director, Father Henry Carr, C.S.B., then Superior General of the Basilian Fathers, wrote the following in a review of the book:

> No man is a prophet in his own country. This is one of the ways of expressing a constantly recurring truth, that one finds difficulty in appreciating another's stature when he stands close. For many years now the Baroness de Hueck has been one of the best known women in America, particularly in Catholic circles. What other women compare with her in prominence?
>
> Because so many saw her, heard her, met her, talked with her, they could not project her, as it were, away from themselves — far enough away to place her on a world map, and even more than that, on the same canvas of history. They could not possibly realize what an extraordinary woman she is. If anyone read a book like this published in some European country about a woman there, he would marvel at one of the striking characters of history. If it were fiction it would seem too much to be true, too impossible. Yet it is not unreal: it is the sober truth.

Who could know Catherine better than her husband, or her former spiritual director, Fr. Carr, one of the greatest and holiest spiritual directors of modern times, or the holy priest who served her so well for 30 years as her spiritual director in Combermere, Fr. John Callahan? And yet, I am convinced that the author of the present book, Fr. Emile Briere, *knew her better than they,* and that this book reveals the real Catherine Doherty better than any other biography ever written, or which ever will be written!

As a young priest of the diocese of Edmonton, Alberta, Father Briere was the founder and leader of the budding apostolate of the laity in western Canada, then known as Catholic Action. He first encountered Catherine in 1936 through the paper, the *Social Forum.* In 1940, he went to New York City and met her for the first time at her Friendship House in Harlem. They spent several hours together (as Fr. Briere relates in this book) discussing the lay apostolate.

In 1953, Catherine was in Edmonton and made a retreat under Fr. Briere's direction. He then asked her to open a Madonna House on skid row in Edmonton, and Marian Centre was established there in 1955. On October 20, 1955, he arrived in Combermere with his bishop's blessing. By the year 1957 he was working closely with her and Fr. Callahan in the supervision and development of Madonna House.

In 1959, at Fr. Callahan's request, Fr. Briere began to accompany Catherine on her frequent visitations of the mission houses, and on all her lecture tours. From January 3, 1977, she became, as he puts is, ''my whole work,'' and from then on he was with her constantly from morning until night. She would often summon him at night when she was in great distress from mystical sufferings or diabolical attacks.

Through a gift of the Holy Spirit, Catherine and Fr. Briere were drawn together in a unique friendship, rooted in the love of Jesus and Mary, a crucifying and glorious incarnation of that line of our little mandate of Madonna House: ''Love, love, love, never counting the cost.''

About the nature of the present book, subtitled ''A Personal Vision,'' Fr. Briere writes:

> Many people will write a biography of Catherine, I am sure. But no one writer or biographer could ever begin to tell her story satisfactorily, let alone exhaust the subject. I am purposely leaving out many details which can best be handled by professional historians and scholars.
>
> I write from my own point of view, which is that of friend and confidant. I have been privileged to associate with her on a daily basis, and have enjoyed her full trust and confidence. I am attempting to share the life of this great woman of God, and how he led and formed her for the work which he asked her to do.

The present book concentrates mostly on the years of Catherine's life before she came to Combermere. But Fr. Briere uses these events to serve as material for commenting on the whole of her life, and her significance for our times. If God permits, he hopes to continue his reflections in another volume, which will deal more with the years in Combermere.

Catherine died in the arms of Fr. Briere on December 14, 1985, the feast of St. John of the Cross. He will relate, the first time in a book, some of the details of Catherine's death; this will be, I am sure, of great interest to all those who know and love her.

Finally, Fr. Briere himself sums up this beautiful little book best of all. Speaking of Catherine and himself: ''The prophet, the visionary, climbs the mountain alone, like Jesus who went out onto the mountain to pray alone. But a friend can accompany the prophet and enter into a similar silence and solitude, making the loneliness bearable, changing it even into companionship'' (p. 166). We who belong to Madonna House and who loved Catherine so much — and, indeed, everyone who realizes her significance for the Church and the world — can never thank Fr. Briere enough for being this friend to Catherine and making at least a little bit lighter the heavy burden which the Lord asked of Catherine — that of being a prophetic voice in our critical times.

Rev. Eugene Cullinane
Priest of Madonna House

Chapter One

I MEET KATIA

It was a soft, balmy, August night in Harlem. The year was 1940. I was just 23, and I had been ordained for three months.

I had gone to visit the Catholic Worker, on Mott Street in the Bowery section of New York City, because I was vitally interested in all things which pertained to the betterment of the poor. Peter Maurin and Dorothy Day were not there, but the atheist who had been my host told me as I was leaving, ''If you are interested in this kind of thing, you just might want to go and visit Catherine de Hueck. She is a Russian noblewoman who is working in Harlem.''

It was just after supper, and night had not yet fallen when I reached Lennox Avenue and 135th Street. I had taken the subway, and had hoped to visit a friend of mine who lived in Harlem, about a mile away from Friendship House. However, he was not at home.

So with great eagerness, joy, and appreciation I walked the streets of Harlem. In 1940, the world was still a fairly simple place to live. World War II had not yet broken upon us. Movies and songs were more gentle and tender — more filled with the promise of everlasting love. One could walk the streets of Harlem without even a thought of fear or of danger.

As I came closer to this place called Friendship House, I noticed how interested the people seemed to be in this young priest dressed in his clericals. I was impressed at how friendly they were. People sitting on the steps of the houses greeted me. They even called me ''Father.'' Many seemed to know where I was going, and little children said: ''It's not far. Just keep going. It's three blocks away.'' Even the grown-ups greeted me with ''Good evening, Father.''

Fearfully I walked in, wondering what kind of a person I would meet. I had heard of this holy woman before, and that was enough to frighten me away. Holiness had often been frightening, but was the frightening kind a true holiness? The Jansenistic ''holy woman'' seemed to me to be far from being truly holy.

As I walked in, I was wondering what this woman would be like. I had heard that she was holy, and dedicated. But I was thinking, ''Is she human? Is she compassionate? Is she merciful? Does she understand the weakness of human nature? Will she be cold, rigid, ascetic, and self-righteous? Well, I can always walk out. I don't have to stay very long.''

I opened the door. She immediately arose and strode over to me with a firm, strong step. She held out her hand and said, ''Welcome, Father. Come and sit down.'' We then introduced ourselves, and she sat down again behind her desk. I sat across from her on a stiff chair, trying to sit very properly before the Presence! My black hat rested stiffly on my knee.

She began to speak about the Mystical Body of Christ. Why, I don't know. My favorite doctrine as I studied in the seminary had been this doctrine that Christ is in each of us, uniting us with himself to the Father, and with each other through the Holy Spirit. I was enthralled by her words, by her vision of faith, and I could realize much more the Presence of Jesus

Christ in each one of us. I could see that Presence in all of the baptized, in all of those who desire to be baptized, in all of those who want to know God and to be one with him. My heart was truly warmed, consoled, and dilated by her words and by her doctrine.

This was a kind of holiness that appealed to me. I knew that I was in the presence of a true, authentic holiness. I knew then and there that the God she believed in was the true God. He was a God of mercy, of compassion, and of forgiveness.

But my first impression of Catherine de Hueck was that she was a poor woman. Here, undoubtedly, was a great woman, and yet what radiated from her was not only the glory of God, but the total weakness and poverty of the human race. It was the poverty of St. Francis. It was the poverty that each one of us would desire to practice if only we had the courage to do so. She reminded me of my good friend, Leon Bloy, and of his book, *The Woman Who Was Poor.*

As Catherine sat there talking away strongly, passionately, intelligently, with an authentic theology, I noticed the tattered, fawn-colored sweater, the old blouse, the skirt that needed mending, her bare legs, and sandals which barely covered her feet. At that moment I knew that poverty, voluntarily embraced for the sake of Christ and for the love of others, that total dependence upon God, was one of the most beautiful things in the world. I also understood deeply that every one was my brother and sister. I understood that the Negro was my brother and sister, that my enemy was my brother and sister. My love for the Body of Christ grew and expanded during those three hours.

It was strange that we should be alone. It seemed as though she had been sitting there reading and waiting for me. It was also strange that not a soul walked

15

in during that time, and the telephone which was usually busy, never rang once.

I smoked in those days, and, in the middle of the conversation, I felt at ease enough to pull a package of cigarettes out of my pocket. I'll never forget it! It was a package of Lucky Strikes and it was nearly full. I said, "Do you mind if I smoke?" She lunged across the desk, grabbed the package, and said, "Not at all." She grabbed one, put it in her mouth, lit it with a determined stroke of the match under the top of the desk, and puffed happily away! The rest of the package she put in the pocket of her miserable blouse! I enjoyed that, and later said to her, "Do you mind if I have one of your cigarettes?" And she answered, "Oh well, alright." Then she carefully took out one and handed it to me. That was my only cigarette for three hours!

I don't know what I loved most about her that night — her humanness or her holiness, her closeness to God or her absolute, downright earthiness. All I know is that I was very glad and happy.

Around 10 o'clock, Catherine felt that I should have something to eat (I was very thin at the time). So we went to her flat which was called "Madonna Flat," and was about two or three blocks away. It was just across the street from St. Mark's Church. I remember that she gave me milk and a sandwich. Then she took me to the corner of Lennox Avenue, and showed me the nearest subway station.

As we were saying good-by, she knelt at the corner of Lennox Avenue and 138th Street with its crowds milling about and, without any kind of hesitation or self-consciousness, asked for my blessing.

I was a brand-new priest, and I believed that a priest's blessing was something very special, but she made me realize how immense and powerful, and how consoling it really is. She kissed my hands — those

16

sinful, earthly, but anointed hands. Because of her faith, the Priesthood of Jesus Christ present in me was impressed into my spirit forever.

I walked away knowing without a shadow of doubt that I had met a person who really knew God. I knew better than ever before that God was wonderful, that God was Father, and Mother, Brother and Lover. I knew that God was LOVE. That strong and deep impression has stayed with me all of my life.

Many people have revealed God to me. I am forever grateful to my many teachers, the priests, the laymen and laywomen who have shown me the face of Christ in one way or another; who have revealed to me the power of mercy, compassion, the tender love, that strong and tender love of our God. But I must testify to the fact that Catherine de Hueck on that balmy, August night in Harlem, touched me as I had never been touched before. She had revealed God to me and increased my faith in him as no one had ever done before.

I left her that evening at the corner of a busy city street. She turned to go back to her modest, little apartment, and all that I saw, as I watched her go, was an extremely poor woman, but one that radiated the power and the glory of our God.

Chapter Two

RUSSIA — KATIA'S COUNTRY

Catherine de Kolyschkine was Russian through and through. She had lived most of her life in Canada and in the United States. However, she always reacted as a Russian. There was nothing Canadian, nothing American, nothing Western, about her; and this presented a mystery.

It always amazed me how Russian she was, in spite of the fact that she had spent only about ten years of her entire life in Russia. As her father was in the service of the Czar, the family traveled a great deal. Her childhood was spent in Egypt, France, Greece, Turkey, and various other places. In her own book, *Fragments of My Life* (Ave Maria Press), and in Father Eddie's book, *Tumbleweed,* this part of her life has been well described. Yet living with her you saw that she reacted as a Russian in everything.

I have often wondered how a person can be so rooted in the spirituality of her own culture — the culture of her origins — when she has lived most of her life in the culture of the West. She has lived immersed in Western spirituality, and Western Catholicism until Vatican II was extremely Jansenistic. I often wonder how a person could have lived through all of this without having been overwhelmed by it, subjected to it, dominated by it. But nothing dominated Catherine. She was a free spirit.

Catherine was the only truly, free spirit I have ever met. I have met a few other free spirits in my life, but she was free with a spirit that knew God even in her darkest moments. When faith to her was as dark as a black stone at midnight on a moonless night, she knew God. She had a discernment such as I have never witnessed in anyone before, and all who knew her would agree to that. Everyone sensed this freedom of spirit.

Yes, Catherine was Russian through and through. Why do I want you to know that she was Russian? Why do I want to talk about Russia so much? Why do I want you to love Russia? It is because Catherine was not just one person. Four thousand years of Russian life have made her the unique person that she was.

We are all the products of a vast physical and cultural inheritance, and it comes out in many ways. Catherine's roots are very deep, in the heart of both human Russia and Christian Russia. It is almost unbelievable. I have known her and lived with her in great intimacy for some 40 years. I have never seen her react, respond, or feel, except as a Russian Christian. She was, however, inserted in the divine and in her own fleshly origins as nobody I have ever known. She loved to have a bit of the soil of Russia in her hands. She was a daughter of that soil. She was a daughter of the marshes as well as of the great forests.

Deep in the soul of Catherine there was a training in a strong, human, fleshly culture and inheritance which related everything to God. The marshes and the forests had brought forth people of deep faith — a contemplative people who were real and human.

Russian history begins only about a thousand years

ago, or perhaps we could say eleven hundred years. If you want to be exact, in 862. For three thousand years, the Russian people lived in the marshes west of the Dnieper River. For three thousand years they were isolated from every other influence. What happened there no one knows, except that a very strong culture was built into their very flesh and bones.

In the ninth century they came out of the marshes. Three tribes emerged: The Great Russians, which was the largest, (today consisting of about 100,000,000 people,) The Byelorussians (about 7,000,000, also called The Palominos, or "white ones,") and the Ukrainians, called "the little Russians," (about 50,000,000). A culture was formed that is one of the strongest in the world.

Catherine was a Great Russian. She belonged to the group of people who moved from Kiev in the 12th century, and trekked north to Vladimir, Suzdal and Moscow, this latter becoming the center of the Great Russian people. They now occupy, with the Indian tribes of Siberia, two thirds of the country.

From the forests and the marshes came certain characteristics which we noted in Catherine. Honey was something which she enjoyed very much. It was the only sweetness the forest people knew. Catherine's great sense of hospitality was deeply bred into her very being. When you lived in the forests and people came to you hungry and cold, you knew that they had nowhere else to go. They were poor, hungry and cold, and they needed you. You brought them to the warm stove, and shared what you had, even though it might be just bread and salt, or, perhaps, soup. You entered deeply into their needs.

Few people ever met Catherine without being offered a cup of tea or soup or whatever else was available. On the first night I met her she offered me food and drink. To know Catherine was to know deep, loving, hospitality — the hospitality of a great and generous heart.

Today, when a person thinks of Russia, he thinks mostly of Communism, of the threat which it presents to world peace. He thinks of the Soviet Union rather than of Russia. It is hard for many to think of Russia with affection, and to embrace it without reservation. The word ''holy'' never seems to come to mind when we think of that immense nation which constitutes one-sixth of the earth's land mass.

But Communism is not the true Russia. The Soviet Union and Communism are a passing blight or sore on the body of Russia. Perhaps a necessary phase in the march of this chosen country through history and towards God.

For many centuries — from the days of its conversion, its baptism under Vladimir at the end of the 10th century, until the Revolution of 1917 — Russia was known to many people as a holy nation. It is most extraordinary, but true, that if you go to Russia today with an open heart, without prejudice, and look deeply into her heart, you will love Russia. To know Russia is to love her.

The real Russia is penetrated completely by the mercy of God, by the love of God for his people. The Russians believe deeply in God's mercy. The human and the Christian have embraced each other in Russia and have become one. In the West, from the Council of Trent until Vatican II, the human and the Christian hated each other. We have suffered from all of this. We suffered from Christianity's sin against the flesh, the body. The body's needs and urges were considered so wrong. Even marriage, with its enjoyment of sex, was wrong. Physical enjoyment was wrong. We forgot that the Lord himself took on our flesh. He felt it all. He *was* it all. He *was* everything we are.

In the West we were dreadfully hurt by this antagonism between flesh and spirit. We suffered an incredible guilt from being simply human, with human desires, psychological reactions, and totally normal human angers and hungers. Russia did not fare much better than we did in this respect, except that the Russians accepted God's mercy! They believed in God's mercy, and worried less than we did about the sins of the flesh. However, they *did* worry much more than we about sins against *love.*

Rarely in the history of the human race has a nation allowed Christianity to penetrate its culture, its human civilization, its atavistic customs more thoroughly than Russia has done. Christians in Russia were able to listen to the Gospel of Jesus Christ in their own language from the very beginning of their conversion. They took it seriously. When they sinned, they called it a sin. When they didn't forgive their brother, they said, ''I am going against the Gospel of Jesus. I do not forgive.'' When they gossiped, they knew they were harming the Body of Christ.

It isn't that Russians have been less sinful than the rest of us. No, perhaps they have been more sinful. Who knows? They love passionately and they sin passionately. Catherine herself is a good example of that passion. She was, in all respects, a passionate woman. Everyone has heard the saying: ''Scratch a Russian, and you will find a Tartar.'' The blood of the Tartars coursed in the veins of Catherine as much as it does in the veins of all Russians. And no one would deny that there has been a lot of violence throughout Russian history. One of the Czars reputedly murdered his own son. One day he would be full of prayer and repentance, and the next he would send some of his enemies to prison and have them killed.

Another characteristic of Holy Russia was forgiveness. The sins of the flesh were the sins of the flesh. But lack of forgiveness was considered a far, far greater offense because it struck directly at the Commandment of Love, which was the Commandment of the Lord.

From the very first days of their conversion, Russians understood that God was merciful and compassionate, and that we should love one another. They understood that we should love the enemy, and even turn the other cheek. Now whether a person actually did it or not, he knew, at least, that this should be done. If he didn't do it, he knew that he was going directly against what should be done. He knew he was acting contrary to truth, and that he was living out of reality. He knew that he was denying the Word of God, hurting himself, and wounding his own spirit. Forgiveness, love of the brother, love of the rejected ones, hunger for justice, all of these made up Holy Russia, and were stamped deeply into the very heart and soul of Catherine.

For most people in the West, Russia begins with Dostoyevsky, and Tolstoy; with Glinka and Tchaikovsky. But, as I have said, the true Russia is hidden in three thousand or more years, and something happened that made them a strong people, but also a people with their weaknesses.

At the end of the 10th century, Christianity came. The greatest of the saints at that time was Theodosius. He was a hermit who lived in a cave in Kiev. It was called ''Cave Monastery,'' because the monks actually spent part of their lives in caves under the ground. Eventually Theodosius built some monasteries above the ground.

Today the site of the Pecharsky Lavra is absolutely glorious. You see an immensity of terrain dotted with golden cupolas, churches and monasteries. You can walk through the caves where there are innumerable bodies preserved for a thousand years. When you walk on the grounds of Pecharsky Lavra, your spirit is raised up to heaven!

Theodosius was given a special grace by God. It was to love the rejects of society, to love the serfs, the prostitutes and the drunks (today it would be the drug addicts). He loved all of those whom society rejected. He lived with them. He appreciated them all. He worked with them. Even when he became a celebrated abbot and a counselor to many famous people, he still used to work in the fields with the serfs, because in them he found Christ. They were the source of his strength, his holiness, and he knew it. He loved and blessed them and was their true servant. This love of the rejected was very deep in the soul of Catherine.

Russia is a country of mysteries. What took place in those marshes for three thousand or more years, and formed the Russians as a people, is a mystery. The work of God in bringing these people to Christianity is a mystery. It has always been a mystery to the West how Holy Russia could have become Communist. Catherine always said that her father could never believe that it could happen, and that he died in Finland from a broken heart. But the mystery which I want to speak of here, is that of God's great gift of faith to these people of the marshes and the forests.

In the 10th century when Vladimir was looking for a religion for his people, he sent envoys here and there to investigate various religions. In the course of their travels, they went to Hagia Sophia, the magnificent cathedral of Constantinople, and there they attended the Byzantine Liturgy. It was the Liturgy of St. John

Chrysostom. He had been the celebrated Archbishop, Doctor of the Church and Theologian, of Constantinople, (today known as Istanbul in Turkey). They reported back to King Vladimir on each of the services which they had attended: the Catholic, the Muslim, the Jewish and the Byzantine. Of the latter they said: ''We thought we were in heaven.'' This is true of the Byzantine Liturgy to this very day.

The advent of Christianity under Vladimir, and the power of Christianity over these people — how they took to it, understood it, welcomed it, and lived it — is incredible! It is true that Vladimir imposed it on them, and forced everybody to be baptized, but that didn't seem to matter a bit. They totally embraced Christianity, especially after they had received the icon of Our Lady of Vladimir. They called it Our Lady of Tenderness. It is most probably because of her that the real Russian is completely penetrated by the mercy of God, and his love for his people.

The real Russia, even in its atheists, is filled with appreciation and respect for the so-called dregs of society. Read the atheist, Maxim Gorky, the hero of the Communists, and see how much he loved the poor of Russia. In Gorky you will find some of the most beautiful passages of Russian literature, especially in his book, *Matushka*, (Mother). One day, he says, men will really come to love one another, and let us work for that.

It is interesting that it was a Greek, Theophanes, who gave Russian iconography its soul. He came from Byzantium; yet, within a few short years he had become more Russian than the Russians. He was the one who taught Rublev and all of the great iconographers of Russia. The first icon that Byzantium or Greek Orthodoxy sent to Russia was the icon of Our Lady of Vladimir. I have mentioned it as being greatly loved by the Russian people. It is an icon of tenderness, where Jesus consoles Mary, and Mary consoles us. This icon had an incredible influence on the Russian people. It was through it that they came to know the tenderness and mercy of God.

This was about the 11th century, so that their first religious knowledge was of a God of tenderness, mercy, compassion and love. In Novgorod you will find some absolutely magnificent frescoes of Theophanes, the Greek who became so Russian. These frescoes are utterly Russian, full of tenderness and mercy, full of repentance. All the eyes in these frescoes are weeping tears of repentance.

It would not be fair to leave the subject of iconography, which is so much a part of Catherine's spiritual inheritance, without elaborating a bit on Andrei Rublev, who was taught by Theophanes and who later founded the Moscow school of iconography, with its center in the Monastery of St. Sergius. Perhaps no religious painter has achieved such a clarity of vision, and been able to capture so well on wood the very spirit of God in Our Lady, in the saints, and particularly in that most famous icon of the Holy Trinity. This humble monk lived and painted towards the end of the 14th century and the beginning of the fifteenth.

When we say "Holy Russia," we mean the culture penetrated by the Gospel of Jesus Christ. We mean the Russians who took their religion seriously, who were faithful believers, who were formed and nourished by the Liturgy, and whose life-rhythms were regulated by the fasts and the feasts of the Christian calendar. Catherine has written well of this aspect of her life in *My Russian Yesterdays.*

Through the prayers of the Mass they learned the mystery that was being celebrated on that particular day. They prepared for those feasts mostly by fasting and inner silence. Parents taught their children to celebrate the great feasts, and thus to participate in a very powerful way in the mysteries of Jesus, of Mary, of the Father, the Son and the Holy Spirit.

Special feasts brought special foods that were pleasant and nutritious, but which also carried a deep symbolism. For instance, the Paska at Easter, made of cottage cheese, sugar, butter and raisins, was pleasant to the taste but it also reminded each one that Christ had risen from the dead, and that Christ himself is the sweetness of life, and that without him there is no life. He is the life of each person. These people lived constantly in the presence of God, the Father, Son and Holy Spirit. Every aspect of life was regulated and *penetrated* by the Gospel.

The Word of Jesus was taken seriously even by those who denied it. The atheists knew how to blaspheme well, just as the saints and the true believers knew better how to sing the praises of God. They praised God in song, in feasts, in fasts, in each other, in the criminal, in the rejects of society, in the ''humiliati,'' in oneself, and in a very special way, in the icons.

The real Russia, as I have said, is completely penetrated by the mercy of God, by the love of God for his people. One could also say that the real Russia is still in many hearts penetrated by love *for God* as well.

One day, when I was in Russia, I stood in the Church of the Holy Trinity in what is known now as Zagorsk (Monastery of St. Sergius). In this church are found the most magnificent religious paintings in the world. They are the paintings of Blessed Andrei Rublev. Yet I saw none of them, because I was transported out of myself into the beauty and glory of God in that church. I tried to look. But in that church there was something far more than paintings by Andrei

Rublev and Theophanes, the Greek, his master and teacher, and all of the holy monks who had lived there. There was the great faith of the people of Russia, and that faith transported me into heaven for a few moments!

When we came out of that church, even my guide was a different person. She asked me about Jesus Christ, and I was privileged to evangelize her for about an hour on the way back to Moscow.

Holy Russia, to know you is to love you! There I saw God and his Love. That I know. Today the best men of Russia are rejected, not by their own, but by the government. Today the jails are full of holy and good men. They are called ''dissidents,'' but they are heroes. Bishops and priests are among them. A part of Holy Russia has remained hidden away within the boundaries of the Soviet Union, and is known as the Church of the Catacombs. Another part of Holy Russia is united to the Patriarchate of Moscow. Since 1917 too, Holy Russia has gone all over the world through its émigrés.

It must be said that we in North America received the very best fruit of that majestic tree in the person of Catherine de Kolyschkine de Hueck Doherty. She was the best of Holy Russia. Catherine was truly Russian. She was a most human Russian. She had no fear of sex, or alcohol, or of the flesh. She had *none* of our guilt. Often she said: ''I don't know what guilt is.'' And it is not because she hadn't done anything wrong! She also did wrong things, but always said: ''I ask God to forgive me and that is the end of it. He does forgive.''

The Holy Russia of St. Theodosius, of St. Nilus, of St. Seraphim of Sarov, Dostoyevski, Tolstoy, and Gogol has been distilled for us in the person of Catherine. She has brought Holy Russia to us. She has passed on to thousands, perhaps millions, of people the very best of the spirituality which was born in the hearts of thousands of saints, and lived out in the lives of millions of people, especially in the last thousand years, the faith which was taught to her by her father and mother. Through her books, through her lectures, and especially through her way of life, she has passed on to millions in the West the very best of Holy Russia.

When we think of Catherine we can only thank God for all the saints, for all the monks, for all the martyrs, for all the peasants, for all the serfs who lived out so well over the centuries, the Gospel of Jesus. I can only thank God for them, and praise him for Holy Russia!

Chapter Three

KATIA'S PARENTAL TRAINING

Catherine de Kolyschkine's origins have been well outlined in the two books I have previously mentioned. I would just like to summarize here a few biographical details.

She was born in 1896 in the town of Nijny-Novgorod, which means "Little New Town." Today the name of that city is Gorky. It was named for the celebrated writer, Maxim Gorky. Today it is famous for its tractor works. It seems that her father had business in that town: he and his wife were going to an Exposition there. Catherine was born in a Pullman car — a significant symbol, as she was in transit all her life!

If there is anything that strikes me about her childhood it is the utter respect of her mother and father for her individuality and her unique personality. Catherine certainly was not an easy child to bring up! In her autobiography she tells about one time when she decided to run away from home because she disagreed with her mother's way of dealing with her. Yet her wise mother never lifted a finger to stop her. She just let her go.

Catherine had a very explosive personality, even as a child. Proof of this has been the violence of her character all through her life. It was not an unbridled violence, although at times it seemed that the Tartar in her was taking the upper hand. She was violent; she was passionate. Yet that violence always crumbled into utter tenderness when she was approached with kindness.

What a father and mother Theodore and Emma were to understand this child so well! I have no words to express my admiration for them. To deal with a child of such energy, such enthusiasm, so friendly with everybody (when they traveled she would be all over the train or ship making friends), to bridle this intensity and yet lead her onto the path of goodness without crippling her personality — this was no easy task! They let her be herself, but this was done in a very natural way. Years later Catherine was to say, ''I thought all parents treated their children as I was treated. I could never conceive of anything else. It was years later that I realized that my parents were extraordinary.''

Catherine's parents treated her as an equal. They consulted her in family affairs, and they never spoke to her in a condescending way. Her parents never seemed to have realized that they had an outstanding child on their hands. We find that they disciplined her well but they let her be who she was. I find that really amazing, as most parents have such a desire to form their children in their own image and likeness. However, in this case we find none of that. We find a type of permissiveness, which is not really permissiveness, but a deep respect for the individuality of the child. We find freedom.

Catherine's mother wanted her to become experienced in all the feminine arts. So she had to rise early and do in the household exactly the same things as the servants did. She would polish copper and silver, clean the house, do whatever household chores needed doing. She was loved, given freedom, but she was trained and given discipline, and that discipline included manual work.

Catherine was truly nurtured by the Liturgy, by the Fathers, especially the Fathers of the desert, and by the very Word of God. When problems presented themselves, her father and mother quoted the Scriptures, the Word of Jesus. They taught her to live according to his Word. They taught her to share, to give, to love. They taught her especially to love anyone who had hurt her. In every problem they presented the Gospel solution. This is what she has always said about them, and the proof of it is that she always lived that out. When presented with a problem, she spontaneously answered from the Gospels, or from the writings of the Fathers. So it was clear she had been brought up that way. Her Gospel reactions were too spontaneous and immediate to have been acquired later on in life. You don't learn that kind of reaction in school; you don't learn it from theology. That sort of reaction practically flows from the subconscious mind: that's your mother's milk mixed with your father's words. She admired her father intensely. He was very intelligent, very understanding of the world, and was a diplomat for Russia. He had money, there is no doubt about that. There is also no doubt about the fact that they were of the minor nobility. Catherine was a noblewoman. They were not of the high nobility, but that doesn't make much difference to me, because Catherine in her person was of the highest nobility. She was noble to the core. When she walked into a room people sensed it. Her father's work took him to such places as Afghanistan, Sudan, Germany, Turkey, Greece, Egypt, and France. But most important of all he was a holy man. Catherine tells about one time when she followed him into St. Isaac's Cathedral in St. Petersburg. She sat quietly in the back and saw that he stayed there and prayed for two or three hours.

For many years Catherine spoke much more about her father than about her mother. I found it most interesting that in her last years the memory of her mother became more predominant in her life.

It happened this way. One day she gave me a humble, little, old icon of Our Lady and the Child. It is one of the icons known as ''Our Lady of the Way.'' Mary is pointing to Jesus as the Way to God, the Way to salvation, the Way to happiness. Mary looks the viewer straight in the eye and says: ''Follow him.'' Catherine gave me this icon, saying: ''The last time I saw my mother was at the train at Antwerp in Belgium. My mother saw me off. She was a very self-sufficient woman. She had come to Belgium and was earning her living in a most humble way. She had a little peddler's cart, and she sold things on the street. She came with me to Antwerp to see me off, and she gave me this icon.''

After Catherine gave it to me I blessed her with it every night. She would say: ''Bless me. Bless me with my mother.'' That was very unusual for Catherine. Then she would bless me with it saying: ''My Mother grant you a good sleep.''

Her mother, Emma Thompson, had two or three miscarriages before Catherine was born. An older sister of Catherine's, Natasha, died as a baby only a few weeks old. So, in a sense, Catherine was the oldest member of this particular family.

Her brother, Serge, was ten years younger, but they were always very, very close. All through life they loved each other deeply. They always kept in touch, and the love between them grew over the years. Serge worked as a tourist guide in Brussels most of his life. He married and had four children. He was a delightful man. He always admired Catherine profoundly, and so did his wife, Joan. When Serge passed away, it happened that two members of the Madonna House Apostolate were in Belgium, and were able to bring back to Catherine two candles from the funeral Mass. This was of much consolation to her, and she placed them behind the picture of Our Lady of Silence in her cabin which we call ''St. Catherine's Hermitage.''

Another son was born to Theodore de Kolyschkine and Emma Thompson. His name is Andrew. He was only three or four years old when the family was scattered by the Russian Revolution. He eventually landed in Cuba where he has become a judo expert and teacher. He married and has two sons. He is much loved by the members of Madonna House.

When one praises Catherine's parents and their training one might wonder, ''Were they really as great as all that!'' I think they were. They knew how to present the Gospel to that child. They knew that God was paramount and mattered more than anything else. Catherine used to say that her father read the Gospels to her, as well as the Fathers of the Church. To train her mind, he made her read editorials, and tell him what they said. We have mentioned how her mother saw that she was well educated in many things both practical and intellectual. It may be extremely difficult to believe that they were so outstanding as parents, but when you see the fruits of that training, you believe!

What Catherine says about her parents and their training *is* true. They formed her as a thoroughly Christian woman. I have never met a woman who was related so well to everything — agriculture, gardens, flowers, vegetables, animals, sewing, arts, handicrafts, to the whole of creation. So, evidently, her parents opened her up to all creation, and gave her a taste for life. I have never read about or heard of any person so involved in everything.

When her brother, Serge, visited Madonna House in the late '60's, he looked around and observed everything, and then we went to Catherine's cabin and sat down. He looked at her and said, "I am proud of you. You have done a very beautiful thing. You have followed the true spirit of our parents. You have reproduced here everything you have learned from Father and Mother."

Tears came to Catherine's eyes. What pleased Catherine most was knowing that her life was pleasing to God. The second thing that gave her most pleasure was to know that she had been a faithful daughter to her father and mother. As we see the fruits of this faithfulness, we can conclude that nothing she says about her parents is in the least bit exaggerated.

Chapter Four

KATIA ENTERS HER COUNTRY'S PASSION

One of the most pronounced characteristics of Catherine de Kolyschkine's life is that she has been deeply involved in all of the major events of this century. She was only four years old at its birth and she accompanied it year by year with all the strength, the passion, the intelligence and the love of her great spirit. She knew one of the most gentle, tender and civilized periods that the human race has ever lived, "La Belle Époque," the days of wine and roses, the days when the people who could afford it, the bourgeoisie, the nobility, lived a truly genteel life.

It is interesting, for instance, to visit and examine some of the hotels which were built at that time for the total enjoyment of the affluent. Those who could afford it were not "bad people," although they could afford it only at the expense of their servants, their slaves, their serfs, and their colonies. Catherine knew this "La Belle Époque," for she lived it from the moment of her birth until the first great catastrophe of the modern world, the First World War, which began in August, 1914.

I spent some ten days in the National Hotel facing Red Square. From my balcony in my three-room apartment I was thrilled daily by the sight of one of the most beautiful buildings in this world. It is the Cathedral dedicated to St. Basil. Not Basil the great Doctor and Theologian of the Church, the Cappadocian. No, but Basil the Fool, who had such an influence that even Ivan, known as ''The Terrible,'' listened to him (and possibly to him alone). Basil lived among the poor. He was dressed in rags and was destitute to the utmost. He was a St. Francis, not in the gentle and enchanting valleys of Umbria, but a St. Francis in the utter destitution, cold winds, snow and ice of the most abandoned districts of Moscow.

I lived, somewhat, the luxury of those days, the days of ''La Belle Époque.'' The dining room of the Hotel National was totally delightful. There were tables set around the dance floor. The ceiling was a complete mirror. The music and entertainment were most enchanting. As I sat there, with Swedish and American businessmen, enjoying good food, I thought of how Catherine was brought up without care, without worry, without anxiety in a world that had been made exactly for her, for people like her; where, it seemed, that she and they would be forever secure. They had money, position, power, friends in court. Often Catherine said that her life divides into two exact periods. The first was a perfect, happy childhood, spent in the bosom of a loving, united family. Obviously, the second part brought her to the cross, and the transition was not gentle!

One day, all of this luxurious living, this security, was shattered. It was like the hand of God sweeping across the face of Europe, as though he was saying he was tired of sin, tired of selfishness. It was as though he was saying to England, to France, to Germany, to Italy, and to Russia: ''Enough! Enough! Enough!'' The people who had had everything no longer mattered.

Their lives were no longer of any greater value than the life of the most humble soldier serving in any one of the armies. With Sarajevo and the assassination of Archduke Ferdinand, ''La Belle Époque'' ended, not with a whimper, but with a bang, and that bang exploded from England to the Urals!

Without that incident, without that War, Catherine would have lived a most innocuous life. Eventually she would have been the darling of St. Petersburg/Petrograd society. She would have been the spoiled child of Russia, having so many talents, and being so easy to love. Without Sarajevo and that Serbian patriot who killed Archduke Ferdinand and brought the downfall of the Austro-Hungarian Empire, Catherine's life would have been ruined.

At least, it would have been extremely difficult for her to have escaped mediocrity. But God struck hard. God chastised all of the colonial empires. God chastised all the bourgeoisie. God chastised Holy Russia for its many sins of injustice. In the midst of all of this, Catherine, this eager, passionate, alive, beautiful, young matron, recently married to Boris de Hueck, a wealthy man some ten years her senior, matured and grew from child to woman, overnight. Her country was at war, and she and her husband responded together.

It is quite a lesson and quite a mystery to ponder that many of the people who were of the privileged classes, did not hesitate in the least to sacrifice their lives for their country! People who had lived in softness and luxury walked without hesitation into enemy fire, and many of them who were young with lives full of promise, died for their country.

Catherine and Boris were right in the middle of it all. Both of them showed great courage; they did not hesitate to face the danger of death. Catherine's father had instilled in her a fighting spirit. He had taught her not to fear. He had taught her that courage does not mean *not* to be afraid: it means not to let your fear overwhelm you; it means to nail your shoes to the ground instead of running away in fright. She faced enemy fire. She was decorated several times for bravery. The medals can be seen at Madonna House, although she has always been loathe to talk about them or to show them off. Catherine, with others from the privileged classes, generously served the peasants and serfs who had served her privileged class for many centuries.

To really know and understand a people, it is most helpful to see them against the backdrop of the times in which they spent their formative years, and to see how God used those times in shaping who they became. I feel it is well here to spend some time on the causes of, and the reactions to, the Bolshevik Revolution of 1917.

Living as we are at the end of the twentieth century, we are growing accustomed to acts of terrorism. During the last few years terrorists have proliferated all over the world. Terrorists, dedicated to the destruction of the world as we know it, of the political systems as we know them, of the financial structure of the world today, are quietly plotting everywhere. Not a day passes, but some bombs explode somewhere, and that act is immediately claimed by a terrorist group, proud of the fact that they are faithful to their work of destruction.

What we see today is not new. It began some two hundred years ago in France, in Italy, in England, in Germany. It began officially with the French Revolution in 1781. L'Ancien Régime was overthrown. It was made up of alliances between king, Church and nobility. The traditional philosophies of the West, especially the Thomistic, were considered passé. A spirit of revolutionary change swept across Europe, across the whole Mediterranean world. It shook all areas of human endeavor to their foundations. There was revolution in politics, revolution in economics, revolution in religion, revolution in science, and revolution in the relationship between people. People began making bombs and exploding them. Assassinations took place here and there and everywhere. Much of this was done under the guise of atheism. God and the Church were being universally rejected, at least in the daily business of secular living. Religion was not abolished, but it was more ''tolerated'' than anything else. Religion became a Sunday affair — a private affair. In the gentlemen's clubs of England one spoke neither of religion, women, nor politics. All of this was considered bad form.

For some 150 years before the 1917 Bolshevik Revolution in Russia, many anarchists had professed a very militant atheism and had dedicated themselves to destruction. Their action was based on this conviction: the present Christian and capitalistic systems are totally rotten, and so powerful that they cannot be transformed from the inside. If something new and better is ever to be born in our society, the only way will be through the total destruction of the power of Christianity and the economic and financial power of the ruling classes and the wealthy.

In 1848 a German Jew, Karl Marx, with a German industrialist, Frederick Engels, published a booklet, entitled *The Communist Manifesto.* This booklet changed the course of our history, and has influenced mankind as few books have ever done. The thesis of Marx is simple, but that very simplicity appeals not only to intellectuals, but especially to those with less education. It says that history can only be considered as a series of class struggles, and progress has been possible only through class struggle.

Looking at only a few centuries before him, he says that in the 11th century the serfs were at the bottom of the totem pole, and the king was at the top. In between there were a variety of classes: lords, dukes, counts, viscounts, vassals, guildsmen, skilled craftsmen, apprentices, peasants, freemen, and slaves. A struggle lasting some two to three hundred years took place. This struggle was between the poor and the rich, the serfs and the lords. The end result, he says, was an amalgam of opposites, a mixture of elements coming from the serfs and from the rich. This produced a new type of man, a new type of class, called the "bourgeois." This meant the man who lived in the city.

The industrial revolution was born around 1750. Steam was discovered. The bourgeois had money, and became an employer. When he hired workers, a new class struggle began. This class struggle will be the last one, according to Marx and Engels. It will be the last one because there will be fewer and fewer rich people and more and more workers. One day the workers of the world will arise, eliminate all of their masters, and take over the factories and properties. Then the human race will enter a millenium — a time of peace, and of comfort. At this time there will be enough goods to share with all of mankind who will become a "classless society." Since class will no longer be fighting class, we will then have peace.

During the 19th century hundreds of young men and women in Russia belonged to secret societies. These were societies of anarchists, philosophers, idealists and many others seeking to change society into something better. Pamphlets and books were being written. All of this was illegal and the Tcheka (the Czar's secret police) had its hands full trying to safeguard the person of the Czar and the property of the rich.

There was a very unfortunate incident committed by a group of young radicals who called themselves "nihilists" (those who believe in nothing). It was the assassination of Alexander II. It was a senseless crime, because just the week before, Alexander had been preparing social reforms for the serfs and for the country in general. This dreadful assassination killed the progress of social justice in Russia for many years.

In January 1905, a group of peasants led by a holy priest, Father Gapon, marched to the Winter Palace across the square in St. Petersburg hoping to have some word with the Czar Nicholas II. He was inside the palace with his family. The priest and the peasants were carrying icons and praying. They were simply coming to visit their Father and tell him of their miseries, and how difficult life was for them. Something mysterious and incomprehensible happened. Suddenly some of the soldiers guarding the palace saw this crowd walking toward them and they must have panicked. They fired into the crowd, and a goodly number of them were killed. This has gone down in history as "Bloody Sunday." After this, anarchists, revolutionaries, and communists were more determined than ever to overthrow the regime by force.

Communist parties were formed. There were the Mensheviks, who preferred change through a peaceful revolution, and the Bolsheviks, who wanted a violent revolution and the elimination of the ruling classes. The Bolsheviks wanted a dictatorship of the proletariat. The Bolsheviks wanted to conquer and eliminate the Czar, the powerful and wealthy, and the Church. They wanted to create their own form of society. The Bolsheviks became more and more dominant until finally they controlled the Russian communist party.

The Bolsheviks were led by an extraordinary man, a truly gifted leader. His name was Vladimir Ilich

Ulianov (1870-1924), but he became known as Lenin. He was a genius. He radiated dynamism, strength and assurance. Had he been a Christian he would have been another St. Paul. He was a dedicated man who had lived all of his life in and out of jails. He was totally dedicated to the messianic evolution of the new society in which he believed, and was willing to suffer for it. Lenin directed the 1917 revolution in Russia. He governed, and was premier of the Soviet Union from 1918 to 1924, the time of his death.

His way of destroying the Eastern Front, where the Russian soldiers were fighting, was to break down completely the morale of the Russian soldiers. He proclaimed that the time had come for the Russian soldiers to receive what they desired most of all — to return to their farms and grow their own food. Food was very scarce in Russia at this time. He proclaimed that he would give to all the peace that they desired, and that he would end the war, and give them food. The slogan was, "mir y kleb," "Peace and bread."

This slogan spread throughout the army and the navy. It spread throughout the cities and the remote villages. Soldiers by the hundreds began to abandon their posts, and to return home. Trains were clogged with soldiers returning from the front. The whole of Russia was in disarray. Nicholas II, the Czar, didn't know what to do. He was caught up in family matters and serious intrigues. A temporary government was established — an attempt at democracy, but it lasted only a few months. Lenin had sown the seeds of disorder, and then took refuge in Finland, leaving the rest to the Bolsheviks in Russia. In October 1917, he returned to proclaim the revolution.

By that time Catherine had been able, with great difficulty, to leave the front where she had served as a nurse. She had also directed soup kitchens. She had grown from child to woman overnight, as it were, but not without danger and suffering. Finally she was able to climb onto one of those crammed trains and reach Petrograd.

She knew immediately that something extraordinary was in the making. I like to think that she was there when the battleship Aurora fired the shot which announced the revolution. She was there when Lenin arrived, and made his headquarters at the Smolny Institute, a famous girls'school in Petrograd. She was there, leaning against a wall (one can just imagine the pain and anguish in her heart!) when Lenin addressed an immense crowd and proclaimed the revolution. She heard him proclaim the abolition of the Czarist regime, and announce the formation of a Soviet government which he himself would lead. She must have realized that she was entering the passion of her country in a different and more tragic way than she had ever done at the front.

Catherine was moved to the depth of her soul. She was stirred by his words, by his passion, by his power, and she was petrified! She knew that evil was at work here, and she realized the influence this man would have. He spoke with the cold and powerful logic of hell. She knew even then that humanity, that the whole human race, was entering into an unimaginable cataclysm, a bloodbath too terrifying to consider. Her whole being cringed before this vision as she listened to this charismatic leader.

On that day two people confronted one another. One was standing on a podium in the fullness of his power and magnetism. He would influence and affect millions of people. Because of him millions would die, even though his purpose was to bring social justice to the poor. At the other end of the square, hugging a wall for support and protection, was an intelligent and

45

strong woman, who also knew that she had to give her life to the poor, as this man was doing; but not through violence and bloodshed. She knew it had to be done through the proclamation of the Gospel, through the mercy of God. She knew it had to be done through freedom and love. She knew that the answer given to her by her parents all her life was the only real answer: the Gospel of Jesus Christ.

Chapter Five

KATIA BECOMES A REFUGEE

God is the Lord of history, and nothing happens without his direct or his permissive will. It is easy to throw a bomb and to believe that you have made a mark on history, or have solved a deep, human problem. Rebels and revolutionaries, terrorists and radicals, are children. They use the "big bang." They think that by creating noise, by killing, by destruction, they will bring forth something good, something healing and beautiful for their brothers and sisters. They are children, and their means are childish.

All revolutions are the works of children and never of wisdom, or of wise men. Yet, within the revolutions of men — if you dig only a few inches underground — you will find the wisdom of God at work. God allows us to be ourselves. So much so that even in our rebellions and revolutions the mystery of his goodness and wisdom are at work just as much as the mystery of evil. God can use even our human weaknesses to accomplish his will among us.

The Russian revolution of 1917 was meant to be a cleansing moment for the whole of humanity. There had been much sin committed by all nations. The Russians knew they had sinned. There had been many cruel czars and unjust landlords. The Russian nobility and ruling classes had been responsible for much injustice, but they *did* have a sense of sin. They had a sense of what being a victim for sin meant. In the Bolshevik revolution of 1917, thousands of Russians allowed God to fit the cross of his Son to the exact measure of their shoulders. They accepted to carry the cross of Jesus for the rest of us.

Millions of Russians had to leave Russia because of the revolution. They lost everything except their lives, their dignity, and their honor. 20,000,000 Russians died under Stalin alone! The concentration camps of Russia have been full of the suffering Christ since 1917. But that is not only because of the sins of Russia. It is also for the sins of you and me and those of the entire world. We witness here in the Russians one of the greatest manifestation of vicarious suffering since Jesus Christ, who took upon himself the suffering of all mankind. They have atoned for all of mankind.

Catherine accepted the revolution. Being Russian she knew that the nobility and ruling class had been responsible for so much injustice. She knew that she and her peers were losing everything they had owned, including their citizenship, and possibly their lives. But she knew deeply in her heart that Russia, in this way, would atone for its own sins and for the sins of social injustice everywhere in the world. She accepted it. She said to herself: ''Yes, it is right that we should suffer. Yes, it is right that we should lose everything. Yes, it is right. Yes, we are part of an immensely important historical event.''

Catherine's life in the days following the Bolshevik revolution can only be described as sheer horror. We see this young woman, who had been married only a few years, who was deeply cherished by her own family, who was the toast of every company she entered, returning from the trenches of World War I. She is tired, bedraggled, dressed in rags. She had experienced every kind of horror, or so she thought. She had seen human bodies hacked to pieces by shells. She had watched men being blown up. She had assisted doctors as they cut limb after limb from beautiful, young and healthy Russian bodies. She had already entered deeply into the passion of her country.

This weary, young woman returned to the city where she had been so happy and so beloved, to find it was now ruled by enemies. She had become an enemy of the people whom she had always loved.

Soldiers in hobnailed boots made frightening noises as they climbed the stairs to her wealthy apartment. They came, group after group. They came like grasshoppers in a rich field of western wheat! They emptied the kitchen of all its wares. They emptied the dining room of the beautiful oak table and chairs. They emptied the sitting room, where so many people had gathered for classical soirees and genteel entertainment. They confiscated the sofas, the drapes, the pictures, the tapestries, the beautiful Persian rugs. Everything went. Within two days the ''grasshoppers'' had made a desert of a wealthy apartment.

Catherine and her husband, Boris, sit on the floor contemplating here and there a few sticks of furniture and laughing hysterically. That which has been is no more.

But there *is* more. New rumors come to them. They hear shots in the street. Friends call them. ''So and so has been killed.'' ''So and so has been taken away.'' ''So and so has been put into jail.'' They know that they must escape. Night comes. What do they have to eat or to drink? They put into bags what has not been taken away. They go to the door. They look back. They see the home where they have been so happy, where they have met so many friends. They hear the joyous laughter of so many social gatherings. They see the intimate moments which they have had with each other, and with their parents and friends.

Then firmly and resolutely they move towards the threshold and close the door. They know that never again will they be as happy as they have been here. They are now refugees. They are now in hiding. Their main concern at the moment is no longer to be civilized human beings entertaining other civilized human being with good music, literature or art. As refugees they now have only one purpose: survival.

Quietly they walk down the steps of their own apartment. They tred softly and furtively as thieves do. They open the door to the street and look about. Thank God, no one is watching! They move towards Finland. In Finland there will be security, refuge, love and friendship. Catherine's mother and father are already there. They walk, they walk, and they walk. During the nights they walk, and during the days they sleep wherever they can find a safe place to do so.

When they reach the border, a hospitable farmer receives them. He allows them to sleep with the pigs. They should be safe there. Catherine and Boris have reached the depths of degradation. But Red soldiers are watching the border to make sure that none of the nobility escape. By some act of God's mercy, they are able to do so.

They finally land in Finland. They go to their own villa there. It is their country house. With hearts full of elation, they say to themselves: ''At last we are free!'' But cruelty of cruelties, they are not! The communists have taken possession of that area. Once again they are prisoners, but this time in their own estate. The worse is yet to come. The long walk to Finland was in vain.

They are in a room with a fireplace, a few forgotten, frozen potatoes, and a couple of windows from which their tormentors are able to watch them slowly starve to death. The ordeal lasts some two weeks. Describing this incident later, Catherine said that at this moment she knew the utter depths of despair. She said that it was her husband, Boris, who proved himself to be the true Christian. She said he encouraged her, spoke the Word of God to her, and gave her strength not to kill herself. We must remember here all that she had been through in the war just before all of this! Shortly afterward, the White Army liberated them.

I have mentioned earlier how the Russian soul understands the forgiveness of God and his wonderful mercy. Catherine always said that Boris not only forgave all of his enemies, but also he never accused or betrayed any of them! I am sure that it was the same with Catherine. Gospel values were so instilled into them by their parents. One always forgave one's enemies.

Catherine had lost so much weight that when she finally contacted her mother in Finland her mother did not recognize her. The saddened woman fed them and brought them back to some semblance of health.

Catherine and Boris then proceeded to Murmansk. For a time she nursed on a British ship. Later they took a British ship to England. Now they really were refugees. They had no country, and they had lost everything except their lives. It was a total dispossession. They knew not what the next day would bring. They were totally poor; totally at the mercy of other people; totally dependent upon the mercy of God through those people. Truly it was a novitiate for the Apostolate God would found through Catherine, and his mysterious will was deeply at work in her.

Catherine and Boris wondered where they should go. They wondered what country would accept them, would become their home. They looked at the map of the world and both of them said: ''Let's try Canada.'' They were attracted to Canada. The reason is obvious: if Russia is the largest country in the world with more than 8,000,000 square miles of territory, and one-sixth of the earth's land mass, then Canada is the next largest country in the world. It has nearly 4,000,000 square miles of territory. To the Russian, space is of great importance. His spirit needs unlimited horizons. He is cramped by any kind of smallness, whether it be physical, moral, religious, intellectual or philosophical. The land, the forest, the rivers are immense both in Russia and in Canada.

To a Russian, snow is exciting, thrilling. For instance, Catherine always remembered, with great glee, episodes concerning the snow. Some of a Russian's most pleasant moments are connected with snow. Catherine spoke of taking part in the troika races, and her eyes used to glow as she spoke of them. Snow is part and parcel of Russian life. They have memories of skating, skiing, the brilliant sun shining on the immense landscapes, giving the impression of a fairyland, gloriously laden with white moss. The forest, after a snowstorm, became a fairyland.

In 1921 Boris and his young wife Catherine landed in Halifax and entrained for Toronto. They created quite a stir in Ontario, because they were among the very first of the Russian refugees. They were well received by Toronto society and assisted somewhat by their new friends. But life was not easy.

Catherine was pregnant, and Boris was ill. Catherine had to earn the living. She took on various humble jobs such as waitress, laundress, store clerk, and, for a while after the birth of her son, she was a farm maid. She worked in Toronto and later in New York City.

In her book, *The Gospel of a Poor Woman* (Dimension Books) she related many incidents of that intensely difficult period of her life.

Her only son was born in 1921. She named him George, Theodore (for her father), Mario (for Our Lady). She brought him up as best as she could under such circumstances. She had to be away from home often, as she was earning the living — such as it was. George was cared for by hired women who were paid a meagre wage, since Catherine herself was earning only eight or ten dollars a week! Catherine was even being asked to be detached from her son; and he, too, had to pay the price of a great detachment because of the work to which God was calling his mother.

Life was never easy for George. His father and mother drifted apart, and he knew the meaning of intense loneliness. Eventually when Catherine left everything to follow God into the slums, she did her level best to see that George was well cared for. Yet, at the same time, this boy of twelve or thirteen knew that he had to give up much, and that family life for him would never exist. This was extremely painful for him, not only at that time, but through the greater part of his life. However, he went to good schools, was a brilliant student, became a financier, married and had a family of his own. He and his family have always been, and always will be a large part of the love and prayers of all of us. He is most beloved of our family here at Madonna House.

As other Russian refugees arrived, they banded together — a small colony of lost souls, bereft of their most cherished possession: Russia! Who loves his country more than a Russian! Who suffers more by being an exile! Catherine was able, with the Catholic archbishop's permission, to collect funds for a Russian Orthodox church. She helped some friends to start a Russian restaurant. She worked from early morning until late at night at every kind of project to support her family, and to help others in need. It seemed that she was destined for a life of poverty and pain. However, in all of this she became a tower of strength to other Russian refugees who looked to her for help and support.

One day, quite suddenly, life changed for Catherine in a remarkable way. Her talent as a lecturer was discovered by a talent scout for the Chautauqua. This was a group which brought good plays, music and lectures to more remote areas of Canada and the United States. It paid well. Catherine was invited to join the group and to speak on Russia. Now she could earn far more to help her family and the poor. She didn't hesitate to accept, and in this way she came to know Canada and the United States at a grassroots level.

She met thousands of people in her audiences, but she also met individuals, because she was often billeted in homes where she was able to listen, observe, watch, and learn from men and women who constituted the grassroots and the backbone of North America. As she came to know them, her love and admiration for them daily increased. She saw the injustices they suffered, the poverty and the racial discrimination. She saw deeply into the heart of this new world to which God had brought her, and in that heart she beheld the pain of Christ.

From a life of poverty Catherine now entered into a life of affluence. She made good money; she was accepted and respected. She had position and prestige. Her reputation as a lecturer reached the director of a celebrated lecture bureau in New York City. Lectures were in great demand at that time in North

America, as well as actors and entertainers. Live entertainment was in great demand in the days before television, when radio and movies were still in their infancy. The Leigh-Emmerich Lecture Bureau hired Catherine at a fabulous salary. Her job was to travel, mostly to Europe, and there hire famous people to come and bring their knowledge to enthusiastic American audiences. In this way this attractive — not only attractive, but beautiful — woman came to meet the great celebrities of the 1920's. She met people such as Belloc, Chesterton, and Bertrand Russell, as well as many other famous writers and lecturers of the time. Many of these people discovered an empathy in Catherine and found a listening heart. They confided their troubles to her as had the people of the grassroots of America and Canada. She was deeply moved at the sadness of so many whom the world saw as successful and happy.

All of these experiences, joined to the pain and suffering she herself had known, helped to form Catherine into a merciful, compassionate human being. If there is anything that can be said about Catherine, it is that she was very merciful. Sins, especially the sins of the flesh, did not shock or scandalize her. However, sins against charity, sins of arrogance and pride, caused her to suffer an incredible agony. Whenever she encountered these sins she wept before the Lord, even as she wept for her own sins.

Catherine was now affluent, respected, sought after, popular, beautiful, healthy and triumphant. She had come to New York City as a pauper, as an unknown, as a reject from her own land. She had conquered New York City and the new land. Now God was about to conquer *her.*

Chapter Six

GOD PURSUES — KATIA SURRENDERS

No one pursues as God pursues. Tell me, reader, why do you read these pages except that God is pursuing you right now? Deny it, if you can, that he has pursued you all through your life. Deny it, if you can, that he has appeared in the strangest corners of your existence. Precisely at times when you thought that you were really escaping from him, there he was looking at you, beckoning you, and wondering why you did not respond.

God is a lover, and like all lovers he is relentless. But he differs from human lovers in the manner of his pursuit. Though his ways are strong, clear and delightful, his pursuit is always extremely modest, humble and reticent. It is true that our God is full of contradiction. The Almighty knocks at our doors as a beggar would. The Almighty has given us free will, and nobody respects that free will as God does. He cajoles, he incites, he draws, he invites; he even threatens with his mighty, natural cataclysms of flood, thunder and lightning, and volcanic eruptions. Yet all of that is simply a call, a beckoning, a pointing towards the direction that we should follow.

It has always amazed me to witness the might and power of God, and then to see his utterly incredible respect for the freedom of his own creature. We are the work of his hands after all. He made us. Of ourselves we are nothing. Everything we have comes from him — everything. We cannot draw a breath on our own. He gave us the lungs; he gave us vitality; he gave us the air we breathe. He has, directly or indirectly, secretly or publicly, given us everything that we have. Yet this very same God stands at the door and knocks. This very same God resorts to tiny hints. This very awesome Yahweh plays for us and uses for our sake — because of our own immense dignity — the tricks and the subterfuges and all the ingenious ways which lovers have invented to conquer the beloved. He has done these things with all of us. He has done them with the saints. The difference between them and us is that they have responded generously to these invitations. At this time God began to use these tricks of Divine Love to conquer the soul of Catherine. He had his work for her to do.

Throughout the '20s, as Catherine was enjoying great worldly success, God would touch her heart every now and then. He would come to her in the most unexpected moments and draw her to himself. He would speak to her heart; and vaguely she heard words of love, and felt the drawing of the Beloved. His words spoke of poverty, of giving up everything for the sake of the Lord whom she had always loved, who had always really attracted her more than anything or anyone else.

The words came in odd moments. They might come when she was riding the subway to her work in New York; as she danced with a handsome man in some wealthy nightclub; as she sat in the privacy of her own comfortable apartment; when she was preparing herself for sleep. The words kept saying: "Come, follow me. Come, follow me. Come follow me."

All these words, as they were spoken in her own heart during the late '20s, have been collected. We call them, as she did, our "Little Mandate." We feel that they were given to us, through Catherine, as the words of the Lord for our Apostolate. They have been printed on cards which other people may obtain and use in their own spiritual life.

Here are the words of his Little Mandate:

Arise — go! Sell all you possess... give it directly, personally to the poor. Take up My cross (their cross) and follow Me — going to the poor — being poor — being one with them — one with Me.

Little — be always little... simple — poor — childlike.

Preach the Gospel WITH YOUR LIFE — WITHOUT COMPROMISE — listen to the Spirit — He will lead you.

Do Little things exceedingly well for love of Me.

Love — love — love, never counting the cost.

Go into the marketplace and stay with Me... pray... fast... pray always... fast.

Be hidden — be a light to your neighbor's feet. Go without fears into the depths of men's hearts... I shall be with you.

Pray always. I WILL BE YOUR REST.

One day Catherine said good-by to her prominent position, to her comfortable apartment, to her fancy car, and began more and more to give herself to the poor, helping in whatever way she could. She returned to Toronto, and there she consulted Archbishop Neil McNeil. She said: "I want to give up everything and go live by myself, according to the manner of my people, among the poor. I want to pray, fast, do humble work, serve the women of the streets and the various families among whom I will live.'' The Archbishop understood her vocation immediately.

There have been worldly bishops in the history of the Church, but the bishops who dealt with Catherine always recognized in her the divine — something different, something holy, something to be respected.

Archbishop Neil McNeil was a wise and holy bishop. He told Catherine: ''You are fifty years ahead of your time. Wait a year. If at the end of that time you still want to go and live in the slums in the simple way that you describe, then you'll have my permission. In the meantime I would like you to investigate conditions in my own diocese in relation to communism.''

Catherine spent that year investigating communism in the Archdiocese of Toronto. Toronto was the center of communism for all of Canada. The communists published their own daily newspaper called *The Canadian Tribune*. Catholics who were aware of the injustices of capitalism had nowhere to turn except to communism.

In *Quadragesimo Anno*, that celebrated encyclical of Pius XI, the Pope said that there is another way besides communism, the way of cooperation. He said that there must be cooperation among government, labor, capital and consumers.

Catherine began to teach these new, vital and revolutionary ideas to the people who came to her house. She organized a study club. She taught the people that the Church was interested in the poor, in unemployment, in people's daily misery. People listened eagerly, and felt a renewed hope.

While Catherine was doing this, she began to give up her possessions one by one. She gave them directly to the poor. She made provision for the care of George, her only child. She put her affairs in order. Then after the year was over, she knelt before Archbishop Neil McNeil, and told him that she still felt the call to go and live among the poor, being poor with them. This time the Archbishop blessed her and said: "Yes, go! Your vocation is from God. You will suffer much."

One day she took a few belongings, packed them into a small suitcase, and walked into the slums of Toronto. Her heart was as bouncy as her step. She knew that she was entering into a tremendous and wonderful adventure. She knew that something exciting and extraordinary was happening.

For a weekly pittance, she had hired a small room. It had a table, a chair, a bed, and a few dishes. That was all. But she walked towards that little room as a bride walks to a rendez-vous with her lover. She walked as a bride walks to her marriage bed.

She reached that poor, little room, closed the door, knelt down, and knew joy as she had never known it before. She knew deeply in her own heart that Christ was there waiting for her. There was no vision, nothing like that. But she knew that Christ was there, and her heart danced for joy. Later in a poem she was to say: "Yes, I would not exchange my wedding day to God... in that gray, shabby room... on that gray, October day... for any other day anywhere."

God had pursued. Catherine had surrendered.

Chapter Seven

BY POVERTY POSSESSED

When Catherine walked into that poor little room in the slums, conditions in Canada were very bad. All of North America, as well as the rest of the world, was suffering from a tremendous economic misery. Since that day in October 1929, when Wall Street in New York City went to pieces, many had suffered great financial losses; some had even committed suicide. For ten years jobs were hard to get, and men walked the streets seeking employment everywhere, but in vain.

It was a most disheartening time. Men lost their dignity and their sense of value. They were thoroughly humiliated by not being able to provide for their families. Women showed wonderful courage in supporting the morale of their men. They invented all kinds of ways to keep the home fires burning. They sewed, they cooked, they took in washing. They did piece work. It is one of the finest characteristics of women that in times of great stress and misery, something in them awakens, and they become in many ways the pillar of the home and the family.

The government was ill-equipped to deal with this cataclysm. Social legislation was an unknown factor in those days. Governments existed mainly to serve the interests of the rich, and to set up the right conditions of tariff, trade, communications, transport, railroads, and the like. These would permit the rich to prosper and to lead comfortable lives. The main function of the police was the protection of property. So the government did not move quickly into this situation.

No one knew that *the first law of government is the care of the poor,* as Pope Leo XIII had clearly pointed out in his celebrated encyclical on the condition of labor entitled, *Rerum Novarum.* This had been published in 1891.

Since the 1750's and the beginning of the Industrial Revolution, the Western world had rested and acted — at times most cruelly and unjustly — upon its own basic principles of economy. These were: free enterprise; the freedom of the market to establish its own wages, prices, conditions of labor; the non-interference of government or labor unions in business affairs.

The poor within an industrial country were known as the *proletariat,* a word which means *childbearers.* The working class existed to produce children for the capitalist's factories. Children were to be hired at the lowest age possible, and given the lowest wages possible. This was known as *the iron law of wages.* The economy was certainly not Christian.

The industrial nations of England, France, Germany, and the United States of America, conquered other countries (which we call today the Third World.) They did this so they could be supplied by these colonies with the raw materials their factories needed. Materials were bought at the lowest prices, shipped to the industrial country, and there transformed into manufactured products, and sold at the highest possible prices. The capitalistic system had produced a great deal of goods at the expense of many, many people. Pius XI had said in *Quadragesimo Anno,* (published in 1931): "Matter enters the factory, and comes out ennobled, but the men who go there are degraded."

It was at this time in history, that God chose to call Catherine into the slums of the city of Toronto that had been much influenced by all of this. Toronto and Montreal were the manufacturing, financial and business centers of a country of some 12 million people. They sold their goods to the Maritimes and to the provinces of the West. Thus, they profited from the other parts of the country. That is why Toronto was, for many years, an unloved city. It was, culturally speaking, an overgrown village. It was generally anti-Catholic. It was only with the coming of the immigrants after World War II that Catholics began to be accepted and not just merely tolerated.

From Toronto, anti-Catholics conducted a bitter and unrelenting campaign. Speakers traveled throughout the country lecturing on the evils of Catholicism. Fallen-away priests were often hired to give their witnesses of the *evils of the Church of Rome.* Indeed, at this time, Toronto was not the kind of city where a Catholic might expect to find understanding or appreciation; it was not a place where a Catholic organization might expect much financial support. Yet this is where Catherine went into the slums to pray, to fast, and to perform humble tasks for others. The bigotry never bothered her. She seemed hardly aware of it.

She, a lady of noble birth, had chosen to become a beggar for Christ. She wrote:

> The first time that you approach a store manager or proprietor to ask him if he can give you any rejects from the produce department, or any broken cans or any pieces of cloth that are not in good condition, you do so with a terrible, hollow feeling inside of yourself. It

is a death. It requires a total emptiness. If ever you may have felt weak and vulnerable in your life before, let me assure you that you have never felt *that* weak or *that* vulnerable as you do now. And of course, the proprietor or the manager eyes you suspiciously. He looks you up and down, wondering what kind of person you are. He wonders what kind of organization he is dealing with. It is well known in the marketplace that everybody has an angle, and that religion is a very good angle. Charitable organizations can also be very selfish and out mainly to feather their own nests. Religious people and people involved in what they call charitable organizations, have often been discovered as frauds, and can be as selfish and deceptive as anyone else. No one blames the manager for his suspicious eye. Yet the effect upon the beggar is frightfully destructive at first. That is, the effect upon an honest, unselfish beggar.

Catherine wrote the above in an, as yet unpublished, manuscript entitled, *History of the Apostolate*. She knew that we, too, would suffer as she had suffered. She was exposed to this kind of shame again and again.

In those first months when she was alone, she begged from local stores. Each day she went out with her basket, begging from the produce department rejects such as potatoes, cabbages, carrots — anything that was going stale or bad. The Friendship Houses founded by her in the States, and all of the houses of Madonna House everywhere in the world, have been nourished through the years, and still are nourished, by the stale bread and rejects from the produce departments of stores, as well as by the financial contribution of friends.

Here let us pause and pray for a moment, for we are touching one of the holiest graces given by God to Catherine: HER PASSION FOR HOLY POVERTY. Like Saint Francis, Saint Clare, Saint Dominic, Saint Benedict, Saint Ignatius, and all of the founders and foundresses of religious orders since the time of Jesus Christ, Catherine was enamoured of poverty. She knew that Christ had chosen to be poor, and that he had come to us in the guise of a poor man. In fact, for God to become man was in itself a descent into the abyss of poverty, the abyss of vulnerability, the abyss of humiliation. He became a tiny seed in the womb of his creature, a human being. Great as a human being is, it is tiny in comparison with the immense God who is greater than the trillions of the galaxies and stars; who is more vast than the trillions and quadrillions of miles which constitute the universe.

Yet the Second Person of the Blessed Trinity had chosen poverty by becoming man. He had chosen to live as the carpenter's son in a humble village. He had little or no backing except for a few friends. During his public ministry he and his disciples lived from day to day by the charity of others. He had no prestige, no position, no money. He allowed himself to be taken captive one day, to be tortured and put to death most shamefully as a criminal between two criminals. The utter poverty and foolishness of Christ is indescribable! It can be contemplated only on one's knees. Catherine was given a great passion for and love of this deep kind of poverty.

Saints have understood that this was the only way by which human beings could be changed, transformed and healed; the only way by which true civilizations could be built; by which men might be reconciled to the Father and learn to love him and each other. They know that programs, even of the highest calibre, do not of themselves bring well-being to mankind. They know that social progress needs a soul, which means a universal change of heart. They know that it is the human heart which must be changed. They know in the depth of their hearts that people must first love God and then one another. They know that the goods of the earth must be shared with everyone.

They know that to fight greed, they themselves must become unselfish; to fight arrogance they themselves must become humble; to fight pride of power they themselves must become vulnerable and have no power. They have discovered the ineffectiveness of human power, of human governments, of human authority, the weakness of human riches. They have understood, as Catherine understood, the power of absolute poverty, of absolute dependence upon God, of absolute weakness and vulnerability.

People in love with poverty appear to us as fools. Their behavior and lifestyle repels us and seems totally ridiculous. We look at them and want to laugh at such stupidity. That is, perhaps, until one day God opens our eyes, touches our hearts, and we see where true wisdom lies. This wisdom is known as the foolishness of Christ. St. Paul speaks about it in 1 Corinthians, Chapter 1. He says:

> For God's foolishness is wiser than human wisdom, and God's weakness is stronger than human strength. It was to shame the wise that God chose what is foolish by human reckoning; those whom the world thinks common and contemptible are the ones God has chosen — those who are nothing to show up those who are everything.

Catherine understood this foolishness, and at an early age she had become totally enamoured of poverty. As she saw atheism creeping all over the world, conquering it, so that even many Christians began to pay only lip service to God, and to act in their lives as though he did not exist, she realized deeply that there was only one force that could stop Marxism, or that more insidious atheism of Christians whose faith was growing cold. Catherine saw clearly that the only force that could conquer Marxism was holy poverty, voluntarily embraced, a total dependence upon God for everything, never storing up for the future. She saw poverty as leaving all in the hands of God, and living upon the charity of others, being always subject to the generosity and kindness of others. What an insight for a young woman in her early thirties!

This love of poverty never diminished throughout her whole life. It grew and grew as others came to join her and embrace a life of total poverty. Nothing caused her greater anguish than evidence of erosion in the spirit of poverty among her own staff. Each one of them can testify to that. Each one can recall many times over the years when she seemed to go nearly out of her mind with grief over the buying of a car or a tractor for the use of the Apostolate, the building of a seemingly unnecessary dorm or a house for guests, or having to buy just about anything, no matter how needed.

Right from the beginning, in the slums of Toronto, Catherine lived a glorious and incredible poverty. So did those holy, evangelical people who followed her to find Christ and to serve him there.

Chapter Eight

FRIENDSHIP HOUSE
TORONTO — BEGINNINGS

What most people would call the knights of the road or bums, Catherine believed were Christ-bearers, so she called them Brothers Christopher. When she and her five co-workers first opened their doors to these men, the house was filled with the radiance of true friendship and love. She had taught her staff to see Christ in all who walked in, and these men soon felt at ease, welcomed and unashamed. Men were traveling back and forth across Canada seeking employment, and the number of Christophers rapidly increased.

Let us look in on Catherine at this time. Can you picture yourself sitting at a desk in a third-rate, ramshackle boarding house, first floor, greeting all kinds of men who come in off the street? Can you imagine yourself greeting them with love, making them welcome in a most expansive way, leading them personally to a humble bench at a humble table, but doing it regally as if you were the gracious hostess of the wealthiest establishment?

I exaggerate not when I say that this was Catherine's way of receiving the men whom many would call bums. She received each as a friend, as a brother in Christ, with great dignity, and so did the other staff.

71

Questions were never asked. Forms were never filled out. Within seconds Catherine herself, or one of the staff, would bring him the ''spécialité de la maison,'' the ''plat du jour,'' the best stew that begging had been able to produce. Catherine saw that all of the houses she was to found later would serve Christ in the poor with the same love and graciousness which she herself had shown.

With Catherine sitting at her desk, hostess to everyone, directing the traffic in the kitchen as well as in the humble dining room, the place was always filled with the presence of God, and with peace and joy. I have never heard Catherine say that she had any trouble with the Christophers, whether they were drunk or sober. I have never heard her speak of them except with great acceptance and great love. I've never seen her act condescendingly toward them. For her the Christopher was truly a Christ-bearer. It *was* Christ who came to dine with her. It *was* Christ who came to give her courage and consolation. I have often heard her speak of pain which priests, sisters, or maybe the staff or I myself had caused her, but I have never, never heard her speak of the Christophers, bums, derelicts, drunks, or whatever you want to call them, except with joy. To her they were always a consolation. To her they always brought a special presence of Christ. She found joy in them, and they found joy in her. Truly Friendship House was a house of friends.

Catherine has written stories of many extraordinary events which happened among the Christophers, not only in Toronto, but in other houses which were founded later. This book is entitled *Not Without Parables* (Ave Maria Press). It also contains many stories about pilgrims in Russia which she heard in her childhood, and which I have heard her recount many times. These stories are all well worth reading.

The Christophers soon came to know that wherever a staff worker of Frienship House walked, there walked a friend; and these men were very protective, especially of the women. This is true today of the Madonna House staff, wherever we are. The holiness and tenderness of Catherine has been imparted to her staff, and is felt by those who are so often rejected. As you read *Not Without Parables* you will see this. You will be entering into the great mystery of God at work in a great person in our society and times. You will also be entering into the mystery of God in the poorest of the poor.

As people began to see that Catherine and her staff served everyone with love, the streets and the atmosphere around Friendship House began to change. There was joy where there had been sadness. There was hope where there had been a gray despair. There was enthusiasm where there had been boredom, sadness and pain. There was joy, laughing and singing.

Children dropped in to visit and to declare there was no God; but returned again and again to hear Catherine speak enthusiastically about God and the things of God. It became necessary to open three or four storefronts for the children's programs alone. They began to know God and to love him.

Others began to see the work of Catherine and her needs, as well as the needs of the Christophers. They began to donate clothing for the clothing room which had been established for all of the poor: the men on skid row, the prostitutes, the families. Staff and volunteers who wanted to have a part in this life all helped in the clothing room or the library, or elsewhere. Catherine begged for everything, and many, many people were helped.

But Catherine was not satisfied with feeding the bodies of the Christophers, or the hearts and minds of the many children who came, or simply giving out clothing. She wanted the whole world to know that there was more to life than the injustices of capitalism and the terrifying repressions of communism. So she organized Monday night lectures on social questions. In the early '30s, Catherine was a pioneer in all of this.

How she discovered the encyclicals of the Popes I shall never know. They were the most hidden documents in the Church. At this time no one seemed to have read these encyclicals, or to have felt any kind of responsibility for justice in the economic order. Today it is very hard for us to believe this, but in those days social justice was a totally unknown quantity. Catherine knew the teachings of our great Popes, and tried with all her strength to make them appreciated, understood, and lived.

To many she was a conundrum, a mystery difficult to understand. What was she doing? Her own way of life was a scandal to the established Catholic Church. Who *was* this woman? She wasn't a religious, and that was the only category people could think of for someone living as she did. Being a religious was an acceptable thing, even to other Christians. Religious women and men were praised and respected. But this woman was totally different. She definitely was not a nun. She smoked, wore lipstick, and behaved as a lay person in every way. There were no restrictions on her behavior, except the Commandments of God, of the Church, and human decency. If ever you could say of a modern prophet: ''She was a voice crying in the wilderness,'' that was certainly true of Catherine Doherty.

The great lacuna in the Church, at this time, was in the realm of social action. Catholics attended Mass, taught their children to pray at home, not to steal, and to be good citizens. And it stopped just about there.

To be a good Christian meant to do these things. Little, or nothing, was known of social justice, of the great need to care for each other in the economic field.

The principle is so simple that I feel like a simpleton in enunciating it: God is the Father of all mankind. He has put into this magnificent earth of ours the power to feed, clothe and to bring a decent standard of living to every creature. If there is injustice, wars, selfishness, it is *our* fault, not God's. We must love one another and share. This is what the encyclicals of the Popes have been about; this is what Catherine was trying to get across at the Monday night lectures. These lectures at Friendship House, Toronto, became an established custom in the various other houses God was to lead Catherine to found.

In addition to the lectures, Catherine found other ways to spread the doctrine of social justice. One of them was a newspaper called *The Social Forum.* This paper lasted only until World War II, but during its brief years of existence it shook the whole of Canada. Its circulation reached some forty or fifty thousand. Many helped to promote it. Fr. Gene Cullinane, a venerable Madonna House priest, remembers how, as a young seminarian in the early '30s, he sold *The Social Forum* on the church steps.

It is interesting and strange how two women, one an exile from Holy Russia, and the other a convert to Catholicism from Communism, became great friends in their crusade for social justice.

Dorothy Day, who founded the Catholic Worker Movement in the United States, was in New York City at the same time as Catherine. Here were two exceedingly great women, each in her own way, working for the poor, for the working man, for a better economic order. Both believed tremendously in the dignity of the human person, and the necessity to obtain for every human being justice and equity founded on love.

It is also interesting how two great women, two giants, appeared on the horizon of social justice while no *man* led the troops. True, Dorothy Day had been formed by Peter Maurin, who had had a great influence on her thinking and in the founding of the Catholic Worker. Yet it has to be said that the struggle for social justice in Canada and in the United States was undertaken by two women: Catherine Doherty and Dorothy Day. Each of them used a Catholic paper (Dorothy Day published a paper called *The Catholic Worker*), but they preached the truth as well, traveling throughout North America. God was evidently in these two women, giving them the strength and courage that they needed. God filled them with faith and hope and love. Each one of them was dynamic, forceful, yet always tender, and as merciful and gentle as Christ himself. Because of their influence hundreds of labor schools were founded by Catholic priests all over America, and these schools saved the working classes of America. Nor did their influence stop here. It has spread and still is spreading throughout the world.

These women gave, not only their teachings, not only their words, not only their material possessions. They gave their *all* to the poor, the neglected and downtrodden, to the great and glorious virtue of social justice. They went to live among the poor as well. They shared intimately the lot of the dispossessed. Catherine was to know this dispossession more and more deeply as time passed.

Chapter Nine

HONEYMOON WITH CHRIST

Now let us visit Friendship House, Toronto, on an average day. Here it is, let us say, 10 o'clock in the morning. You've heard of this Russian noblelady. Her great-grandfather was given titles of nobility by the Czar in 1865, so she belonged to the lesser Russian nobility. You have heard that she is living in the slums, and your heart has been moved and your interest awakened. So here you are ready to meet this woman.

You walk in, and what do you see? This first room is a library. At the desk sits a woman with golden hair. She is busy on the telephone. She ends the conversation as quickly as possible and rises to greet you most warmly. She says, ''Is there anything I can do for you?'' You reply, ''Yes, I would like to know about you and Friendship House.''

Immediately she launches into a broad explanation of the works of mercy, of the needs of the poor today, of the joy of serving Christ in the poor. For her these are obviously not merely words. She lives and breathes the joy of serving Christ in the poor.

You notice a tiredness around her eyes, and a tender kind of deep sadness as well. It is a sadness which never quite leaves her; yet you may not notice it at all because she radiates such joy, such confidence, such warmth, tenderness, and faith in God. But there is an immense tragedy going on within her. The tragedy is this: God is offering his love to us and we are refusing it. Catherine experienced this immense misery all of her life, without surcease. It seems that her main work and purpose in life has been to suffer deeply at the "sight" of God's immense love for mankind being refused by so many of his children. At times this vision seemed unbearable, and she had to shout out to all and sundry on the public platform, or in the privacy of a little room: "God loves you! Love him back by loving one another!"

Catherine offers to take us on a tour. She shows us the many books in the library which have been begged for, and which the men are reading as they wait for lunch. She would always have libraries in her houses. She shows us the kitchen where the stew is being prepared, the clothing room, the rooms where the children's programs take place. She tells you about the religious programs in which they are taught about the existence of God and his love for them. She explains that they are very busy, but that they draw their strength from the morning Mass which they all attend. She often told us, "You can endure anything between two Masses." The Lord is truly her strength and the strength of her staff.

Now the tour is over, and Catherine brings you back to her desk in the main house. She says, "Would you like a cup of tea?" And as you sip the tea, she asks you, in a very discreet way, about yourself. "I think you are a seeker. I think you are looking for God. I'll pray that you find him." How often she was to say this, to thousands of people!

You find yourself pouring out your heart to her about your dreams, difficulties, and misconceptions about God. She observes that in North America, Jansenism and Puritanism have formed a very guilty conscience in us. As you listen to her, you discover the mercy of God. The God *she* speaks about is a forgiving God who has absolutely no use for guilt. She says: ''People should just go to Confession, say they are sorry, and forget it. God has forgotten it. His arms are open to you. Why do you turn away from him? He loves you. Why do you turn away from his arms?''

While you are there, a priest walks in, and you notice that priests also come to Friendship House. Catherine greets him warmly and kisses his hand. You see the tremendous reverence she has for priests. You decide to sit in a corner for awhile and merely observe. You see how she lights up again as she talks with this priest. As you sit there, you hear the priest making objections like this: ''But, Catherine, this is a very unusual type of life. Why don't you become a nun? This kind of life is unknown in the Catholic Church. You're just encouraging people to become lazy. You're condoning sin. These young men and women who follow you might better serve the Church as priests, brothers and nuns. Frankly, I think you are doing more harm than good.''

Many priests came to Friendship House, but not all of them were critical. Some were wonderful friends, and many priests have come to Madonna House itself, and to all of our houses throughout the years. But the foregoing words and similar accusations were leveled at Friendship House and at Madonna House up until Vatican II, in 1962. From then on attitudes changed radically and priests and religious who had criticized Catherine came to see that she had been a prophetic person. She had been a sign of God pointing towards the future, and preparing the Church for the renewal which would come at the end of the century.

But for thirty years she lived this life knowing that at any moment the Chancery Office of the Church could call and say, ''Your work is ended in this diocese.'' This state of complete dependence upon God, of total uncertainty, lasted until 1960 when Bishop William Joseph Smith of Pembroke, gave Madonna House's women's branch legal status as a Pious Union in the Church. But for thirty years she never knew, from one day to the next, whether her work would go on, or be stopped.

Catherine was always busy about many things, but about nothing more than her own spiritual life. She has written extensive diaries — a spiritual journal — over some sixty years of her life. These diaries show a burning desire to be faithful to God, to know him, to listen to him, to obey him, and to follow him by total service to her neighbor. Here are a few extracts from that very intimate story:

February 20, 1927: At Communion today I prayed for George's health. [George, her son was quite ill. Catherine asked God to take care of him and make him well, but most of all for God's will to be done.] Honor to the Blessed Virgin and to the Trinity. I also offered this Communion for Jews. Virtue: submission to the will of God, and to live day by day. Resolution: to really live day by day.

April 5, 1927: Meditation on the Passion of Christ. Jesus Christ in prison. Resolution: count yourself as nothing. Desire immolation of self. Visit Jesus Christ in the tabernacle of your heart. Examen of conscience: self-praise, too much talking.

October 13, 1932: Virtue: absolute silence under undeserved criticisms... to submit generously to all hurts from superiors and others. Ejaculation: ''O Jesus.'' Examination of conscience: spoke unkind words of others, and had a moment of anger under provocation.

October 15, 1932: Examen of conscience: little lies of exaggeration, impatience, desire for good food. Prayer: "Teach me to bear the burdens of others when they cannot bear it for themselves." Virtue: fortitude. Ejaculation: "O Lord, by my strength."

July 3, 1933: Meditation: "Let him that thinketh himself to stand take heed lest he falleth." Resolution: To be humble, to have a low opinion of myself, to cultivate silence. O Jesus, help me! Virtue to cultivate today: humility. Ejaculation: "Jesus."

I have quoted only a few minor excerpts from Catherine's spiritual diaries, but just these few show her resolve to seek God, and to do his will. She desires to do this even though it is doing violence to herself in the process. She knows well that the kingdom of heaven is conquered only by such violence. These diaries are extremely precious, and undoubtedly constitute some of the very best things she has written. Eventually when God seems to indicate it is time, they may be made public. There are several books contained in these extraordinary accounts of the relationship of one person with her God and with others.

I've had the privilege of asking Catherine herself about those early days in Friendship House, Toronto, and I share some of this with you:

Fr. Briere: What were your dreams, your hopes, your feelings, your expectations, as you began the first stages of your romance with God in the slums of Toronto during those days of the Depression of the '30s?

Catherine: Because I am a Russian, the first thing that I did when I came to my little room that I rented for a dollar, was to dance. I danced like David danced before the Lord. After I finished dancing, I realized that at long last I was here! To me *here* meant Nazareth. All through the years when I had money and the rest of it, I was reading the Gospel. I read especially the Gospel of the rich, young man. My dream, my hope, my love and my faith rested in Nazareth. I never visualized Nazareth as it is today. I always visualized Nazareth as it was in the time of Christ. I was young then, you must remember, and I felt that Christ was young too, and the two of us were walking and talking together.

I had hopes of creating a Nazareth in my heart, because I thought in my youth, and I still think so, that Our Lady always had a jar of cookies for the poor, little children of Nazareth, and that she always had time to talk to them and to everyone who came to see her. My hope was to create in my heart a Nazareth with a cookie jar that never got empty. Its true!

In a way, I cannot say that I had too much faith or too much hope. What I did have was too much love, if you can say that anybody can have *too much* of love! There was in that little room of mine love that you could cut with a knife. I didn't realize this, but people sensed it. If they were Russians or Ukrainians they would look for an icon which I did not have at the time and say: ''Well, Our Lady must be near. There is such peace here.''

A strange thing about this whole affair is that I never thought of tomorrow. Why should I worry about tomorrow? Tomorrow would take care of itself. So I just let it take care of itself. Perhaps that was a hope; only I didn't think of it as hope. I think it was faith. It's very difficult, you know, to separate hope, faith and charity. I think it was very profound faith. Tomorrow never bothered me.

There was laughter; there was dancing; there was the dream of Nazareth; and there were days of tears. Because I am Russian I used to lie on the floor, and I would cry. I would cry on it because I had not given up everything. I would cry about many family affairs. Things I had suffered would come back to me. I cried many tears on that broken linoleum floor. It wasn't easy, but it wasn't meant to be easy.

Love of God began to grow again, and in my old book, which was practically in pieces, I read again and again about the rich young man. I felt that he was very poor, and I was very rich.

I thought of how this strange life of mine was like a tree. I have always thought of my life as a tree. I still think of it as a tree — the tree of faith. Whenever it became very difficult, as it did many times a day, with people throwing you out, refusing to help you, police-men questioning you, and other difficulties arising con-stantly, there was always the tree of faith. You could lie under its shadow — it was a lovely shadow. Winter and summer it had a particular mystery about it. It was green all year round — this is how I saw it — and it had immense branches. It embraced me and I felt renewed. I could face another day.

You ask me what were my hopes. I can't answer that. Every day was a gift of the Lord. When you receive a gift from the Lord on Monday, you are not sitting there waiting for Tuesday to arrive; you are so happy that you have received this gift from God on Monday.

My desire was to live part of the time in silence, but to speak as charity dictated and to beg. There was always a dream in my heart, and it was that I would help priests. What else do you want to ask?

Fr. Briere: That is the essence of what I have seen in my own heart whenever you write or speak about these days. It was truly a romance with God. It was not a luxu-rious honeymoon but a honeymoon of utter poverty.

Catherine: That's understandable. How could there be a luxurious honeymoon with Christ? If you put the word 'luxury' and Christ together there is no honeymoon. It's an impossibility. I was a pauper with Christ.

Romance with him is a very strange romance. He is always absent, yet he is always present. It's the greatest mystery that ever existed. The romance of a soul with God is one of the greatest mysteries of the universe. It is a mystery that no one can fathom. The Lord takes those whom he loves to a garden enclosed and there are no keys to that garden.

Fr. Briere: Those first days in Friendship House, Toronto, were days of honeymoon. Then the Lord said: 'Take care of My children; of *our* children. I will give you children now. I will make you fruitful.' We now have spiritual children.

Catherine: Well, when three men and three women arrived to join me I refused them. I had had no desire to start any kind of community. That was imposed on me when Archbishop McNeil said: 'Of course you must take them.' So in obedience to the Church I took them. I realized that God was making me fecund. I also realized another thing: this was just the beginning. There would be many children.

What I didn't realize was that there would be priests coming to join us. I think that because of the great desire I had that my son George would be a priest, the Lord gave me this gift. I now have many sons who are priests. But in the early days many priests did not like us. The less said about that the better.

We called our group a family. I never call it a community; it is a family. And as that family grew, I realized that with the advent of the family, I was entering into the pain of Christ.

Fr. Briere: The honeymoon was over.

Catherine: The honeymoon with God is never over, Father. It is always there. The honeymoon with God continues even while you are crucified, because those who love him are crucified on the other side of *his* cross.

Those of us who know Catherine Doherty well, or even fairly well, would not hesitate to characterize her as Lady Pain. Catherine Doherty has embodied the very pain of Christ himself. I have lived at Madonna House, Combermere, since 1955, and have known her well. In my mind's eye I have seen her as completely draped in blood, with her flesh hanging in pieces. This may sound very naive and dramatic, but I would swear before any tribunal that Catherine Doherty has suffered the very pain of Christ over mankind. She has experienced this pain every single day for all the years that I have known her, and, of course, many years before that.

She has lived every day of her life in exceptional pain and awareness of the misery of the human race, of our rejection of God, and of the pain of Christ, who, as Pascal says, is in agony until the end of the world. Her childhood might be an exception to this, but even then she was very aware of pain in others.

But that pain has known moments of intensity which are beyond description. One of them I am now going to relate.

In 1937 I visited Friendship House, Ottawa (Catherine had founded houses in Ottawa and Hamilton as well as in Toronto). I was told by Father O'Neill that Catherine had left these houses. She had left the *Social Forum* as well. All of these were immensely precious to her. She had left! Where had she gone, and why?

Let us start first with ''Why.''

I have heard her speak many times about why she left Toronto. She has also written about it in her book, *Fragments of My Life,* and more extensively in ''The History of the Apostolate.'' The reasons she gives are, to me, very unsatisfactory. For instance she will say, ''I left because I was accused of being a communist, and all support in Toronto ceased; so I had to go.'' Or she would say, ''The parish priest was very inimical to me, so I had to go.''

Now I do not doubt the validity of her explanations, but I think that the reason why she had to leave Toronto is far deeper than the likes and dislikes of men.

Those are superficial reasons. There is a much deeper one. It was God who called her to leave and to begin again to walk in total faith. *It was God.* It was the Holy Spirit, the Crimson Dove, as she calls him, who picked her up and sent her off somewhere without seeming rhyme or reason.

Have you ever watched a leaf caught up by the wind? Have you ever asked yourself how that leaf feels? The wind picks it up, drops it, and lets it lie there unattended until it is picked up again by the wind and driven into the sky to fall again somewhere. So the Holy Spirit dealt with Catherine. She may give the reasons why she left Toronto, but they are not the real ones.

When she left Toronto where she had so many roots, so many friends, and a flourishing Apostolate with sister houses in Ottawa and Hamilton, she truly had to trample on her heart. She didn't realize this at the time. She had worked so hard to develop Friendship House, and suddenly it was all taken away from her — that work she had entered into so gloriously and enthusiastically.

She began to feel an extreme rejection. She began to know in the depths of her spirit the rejection of Christ in Gethsemane. She experienced, as fully as a human being can, the desolation of not being wanted by the people you love so totally, and in such a childlike way. I feel that this is why she felt in her heart that she must leave. Rejection can cause such pain!

Catherine could not see this at the time, but it is clear to us what God was doing. For when you live with the saints, what do you see? You see the Lord Jesus Christ shaping, forming, tracing his own image upon them. You attend a drama which you cannot compare with anything else in this world. You witness the action of God in a willing person whom he has chosen to draw to himself; a person who is, in her utmost being, the theatre of his activity among men. You see someone who is not only the carrier of his mercy, the bringer of his peace, the healer, the prophet, but most of all, a person in whom we witness the incredible love affair between Almighty God and his own creature. Catherine gave her reasons for leaving Toronto, but we now see it as the action of God who was launching her into a much wider sky.

Chapter Ten

INTERRACIAL APOSTOLATE
AND MARRIAGE

Catherine was fairly famous in North America, and when Father Theophane Maguire, C.P., editor of *Sign* magazine, that most prominent periodical, heard that she was ''free,'' he invited her to cover Europe. Catherine looked upon this offer as a real godsend, an act of the special mercy of God. The pain of rejection so filled her heart that she sorely needed something challenging upon which to focus all of her attention. Rejection, to her, was a total mystery; she never could understand why anyone could reject her when she loved people so deeply. Now she would face the beautiful, the exciting, the tragic, and God would use it to heal her.

Catherine went first to Spain. In 1937 a most brutal civil war was raging there, and she covered that for *Sign* magazine. She saw how people who loved the Church had been hurt by the infidelity of priests and nuns. She saw them turn upon the Church and tear it apart as though they were wild beasts.

She went to France where she visited the various groups of Catholic Action. She reported on the wonderful work being done by Canon Cardijn, a Belgian priest who did much to bring Gospel values into the lives of ordinary people. She saw wonderful, healthy, spiritual things happening in France through these movements, and in the realm of the theatre. She met some of the great theologians and philosophers of the day. She rejoiced at what was happening to the Church in France.

Catherine went to England, to Belgium and to other countries as well. She has written about all these exciting and sad experiences in her book, *Fragments of My Life.* There one can read about them in more detail.

This assignment to Europe did much to heal Catherine from the rejection she had suffered in Toronto. It rejuvenated her spirit. In Brussels she had had a very special visit with her mother with whom she had a strong bond of affection. That was a healing and deep sharing about which she was ever reluctant to speak or write. God had indeed been merciful.

When Catherine returned from the assignment in Europe, there was a great surprise in store for her. There was a letter from Fr. John LaFarge, S.J., a pioneer in interracial justice, inviting her to open a Friendship House in Harlem. This was a section of New York City where mostly Blacks lived. The invitation amazed Catherine, and she was delighted beyond words. She, the rejected one, had been accepted again, and God had asked her to go and love his people in Harlem.

It was with a firm step and a most enthusiastic heart that Catherine walked into Harlem one cold day. It was February 14, 1938 — a day she would never forget. She carried a small suitcase and a typewriter. She had only a few dollars in her purse. But this forty-two year old woman was bursting with love, with joy, and with expectation, as she walked to a destiny that she could not possibly have imagined would someday be hers.

For her work Catherine was able to rent a storefront on 135th Street near Lennox Avenue. She found a little apartment for herself across from St. Mark's Church on 138th Street. It contained the minimum, for which she was grateful. As she walked up the staircase, her nostrils picked up the smell of urine, and she knew she was where she belonged. She had wanted to share the lot of the very poor.

Bishop Fulton Sheen, famous for his radio talks at the time, once said: ''When we meet a poor family, we decide to give them a few dollars or a basket of food. When a Russian meets a poor family, he goes and lives with them and shares their life.'' This was certainly a profound and true statement to make about Catherine de Hueck.

In those days the very expression ''interracial justice'' was unknown to just about everybody. Father LaFarge and his group published a magazine called *The Interracialist*. Of course there was Dorothy Day in the Bowery, and she opened her doors to all. However, when Catherine went to Harlem, it was the first time that a white person had completely identified herself with the aspirations and sufferings of the black people of America; but she herself did not realize this at the time. She, a white woman, walked into Harlem with great enthusiasm, grateful for the acceptance of the Catholic Church she loved so much, but which had not always treated her well.

Harlem, to most of us, is a mysterious part of New York City. Who knows the spirit and soul of Black people? But Catherine walked into this Black world, lived in it, conquered it, as a child walks into a park without fear of what might be lurking in the bushes. Catherine's life in Harlem can be counted among the acts of martyrs, except for the fact that she has never looked upon herself as a martyr. She truly went there as a child, naive and trusting in God. She conquered all hearts, even the hearts of those who might have killed her. She exposed herself to death, but death never came. She exposed herself to rejection, but the Blacks never rejected her. On the contrary they became her friends and defended her at all times.

She has written about her intense loneliness in Harlem, but it was not, in any way, due to the way the Blacks treated her. It was the white people who could not comprehend why a white woman would go there to live. They accused her of being a ''nigger lover.'' Even the Religious of that time could not understand her being there. She was exposed to great misunderstandings, and those caused her great loneliness. I don't believe that Catherine ever suffered a greater loneliness than she did in Harlem. She covered the area with her love, and accomplished great things for the souls of men, but the cost was this loneliness and misunderstanding.

Because Catherine has written a lot about these days in her books and articles I will not go into details here. I will just mention briefly what life was like and the principles for which Friendship House stood.

Here, as in Toronto, Catherine rented storefronts from which to operate. She organized youth groups, a clothing room, fed the hungry, was a friend to the prostitutes, to the Christophers, to the very poor and destitute. She organized a library and encouraged people to read books. She fought the communists who were trying to make converts in Harlem.

Hundreds were touched by the love, tenderness, and care of Catherine and the staff who, inspired by her example, came to give their lives to the poor and to interracial justice. Many others came to witness the work there, and went away inspired to do more themselves.

Catherine may have spent the night, which she often did, crying out to the Lord for mercy, for help in her great loneliness; but morning brought early Mass at St. Mark's Church, and renewed energy.

Catherine had an incredible energy, and love flowed over the entire neighborhood around her. She still found time to lecture all over the United States. She lectured on the most unpopular subject of the times: interracial justice. I believe that she spoke to every Catholic College in the United States of America.

Catherine also founded a newspaper, the *Friendship House News*. It is still well worth reading. Here is an excerpt from the December, 1943 issue. It is a powerful clarion call to interracial justice:

Manifesto of Friendship House

WE BELIEVE:
In the sublime doctrine of the Mystical Body of Christ — for he is the Mystical Vine, and we are the branches. He is the Head and we are the members.

WE BELIEVE:
That the fruit of the Incarnation and the Redemption is the Brotherhood of Man under the Fatherhood of God.

WE BELIEVE:
That faith without works is dead, that we ARE our brother's keeper and have a PERSONAL responsibility therefore, before God, for the welfare of that brother in Christ, and this embraces all men irrespective of race, nationality or color... for Christ died for all mankind.

WE BELIEVE:
That all men are born equal before God.

WE BELIEVE:
In the natural and supernatural dignity of men as children of God, created in his likeness, and possessing

inalienable rights to life, to work, to marriage, to a decent upbringing of their children, and to the pursuit of happiness.

WE BELIEVE:
That a modicum of material necessities is essential to the practice of virtue.

WE BELIEVE:
That the unit of society is the family whose rights precede those of the state.

WE BELIEVE:
That a lasting social order and peace will be achieved ONLY by a Christian Social Order based on Christian Social Justice which includes Interracial Justice.

Because of these beliefs, FRIENDSHIP HOUSE is dedicated to the actions flowing from them, as well as to the integration of those beliefs into the reality of their living. And into that of as many Catholics as they can reach through prayer, example, indoctrination, and dissemination of knowledge in all pertinent phases and all available fashions, as well as through the Corporal and Spiritual Works of Mercy.

BUT...

AS LONG AS THE NEGRO IN AMERICA HAS TO SUBMIT TO THE UNCHRISTIAN, UNDEMOCRATIC LAWS OF JIM CROWISM AND SEGREGATION... Friendship House has work to do.

AS LONG AS THE NEGRO IN AMERICA CANNOT VOTE... Friendship House has work to do.

AS LONG AS A NEGRO IN AMERICA HAS TO LIVE IN GHETTO-SLUMS... Friendship House has work to do.

AS LONG AS A NEGRO IN AMERICA IS REFUSED A BED IN A HOSPITAL BECAUSE OF COLOR... Friendship House has work to do.

AS LONG AS A NEGRO IS REFUSED ADMIT-
TANCE TO A PUBLIC OR PAROCHIAL GRADE
SCHOOL, HIGH SCHOOL, OR COLLEGE, BECAUSE
OF COLOR... Friendship House has work to do.

AS LONG AS A NEGRO IS REFUSED A JOB IN
AMERICA BECAUSE OF COLOR... Friendship House
has work to do.

AS LONG AS A NEGRO IN AMERICA IS NOT
TREATED AS OUR BROTHER IN CHRIST, AND A
CHILD OF OUR FATHER WHO ART IN HEAVEN, OR
GIVEN HIS DUE DIGNITY AS A MAN, AS WELL AS
HIS JUST AND DEMOCRATIC RIGHTS... Friendship
House has work to do.

This is our MANIFESTO. This is our Creed. It stems
from the CREDO of the Most Holy Roman Catholic
Church of which we are the obedient children who have
dedicated our lives to the Integration of the Credo into
the American way of life. Amen.

This was a radical Manifesto for those days.

Men and women from the Catholic colleges in New
York often came to spend a few hours volunteering
at Friendship House. They wanted to give the best of
themselves to Harlem. I have mentioned that many
visitors also came to see the work going on there. One
of these visitors was to become an important part of
the Apostolate.

It was in the fall of 1940 that the celebrated newspaper reporter, Eddie Doherty, came (much against his
will) to interview Catherine about Harlem. He had
heard it was ''the most wicked city in the world.''
Eddie promptly fell in love with Catherine.

Catherine had given up forever any idea of mar-
rying again, even though, after she and her former husband had become estranged, they were eventually
granted an annulment by the Church, and she was free

to do so. When Eddie came into her life, she couldn't believe that this friendship was from God. She thought that she would forever be alone, unprotected, vulnerable and constantly wounded.

Gradually she fell in love with Eddie who pursued her with the desperate passion of a man who cannot be denied. Catherine finally began to see God's hand in this love and accepted it; but it took three years of comings and goings, of joys and sorrows. It took three years of incredible agony on both sides.

Finally they decided to rest their whole case in the lap of a benevolent bishop who was a friend of both of them. He was Bishop Bernard J. Sheil of Chicago, one of the great bishops in the United States during the '40s. His judgment was extremely wise. He said to Eddie: ''You can marry her if you give up everything, and decide to live in poverty with her. Her vocation is poverty. Do you want to do that?'' Eddie replied: ''With all my heart I do.'' The Bishop then added: ''The needs of the Apostolate come first. When Catherine has to go somewhere for the Apostolate, you must let her go.'' And Eddie said: ''I will.''

On June 25, 1943, Catherine de Hueck was wedded to Edward J. Doherty. The ceremony was performed by Bishop Sheil in his own private chapel. Now Catherine's life knew a strength that she had never known before. Eddie became the root and foundation of a new life. Before his coming into her life, she had felt totally vulnerable, weak, overwhelmed by the opposition that she had met. Now she had a protector, a defender. Now the Irish priests spoke to her with a much greater deference and respect! She was now *Mrs. Doherty*. No one could hurt her as she had been hurt. Her apostolate, her intentions, could not be misconstrued again.

Eddie's own story has been told by himself in a

famous book entitled *Gall and Honey.* It is really the story of his immense love for his first wife Marie, and then for his second wife Mildred. It ends with his return to the Catholic Church shortly before his meeting with Catherine in 1940, and after twenty years of anger.

What a marriage this was! Here was the greatest reporter in America and the greatest woman in America living in Chicago in splendid poverty. Eddie embraced poverty totally when he married Catherine. The two of them were united, not only in heart and flesh, but in something far deeper. We witnessed their union over many years, and none of us can express their marriage in words. The depths of their love, their self-giving to the Apostolate, and their self-denial, was a constant model and inspiration to all of us. Their love for God and the Apostolate always came first, and their love for each other, or any manifestation of it, came second. That they loved each other infinitely and incredibly we have all witnessed through the years.

The work of Friendship House continued to grow, and other houses dedicated to interracial justice opened. There were requests to lecture on this vital subject, and Catherine covered the continent regularly every year. She traveled from north to south, and from east to west. She spoke mainly at Catholic colleges. Catherine has written quite extensively about her experiences while lecturing on this unpopular subject. She tells about them in *Fragments,* and in her other writings.

In 1946, differences appeared between Catherine and her staff. These were so pronounced that she felt no longer needed or wanted by Friendship House U.S.A. She has given many reasons for this. She has said there were differences of opinion concerning the democratic process in an organization such as Friendship House. She has said that it concerned the group's desire to limit the Apostolate to interracial justice alone — and various other reasons.

Now all of these factors are true, I am sure, but again I see the hand of God leading her to a more extensive field of the Apostolate.

Had she remained in the United States in the Interracial Apostolate, who knows what would have happened to Catherine Doherty! But she didn't remain; she was drawn by the hand of God to leave the United States and go to Canada. Bishop William Smith of Pembroke, Ontario, had talked with Catherine and Eddie about opening a house to serve the rural poor in Combermere. That had been on August 15, 1945 (V-J Day), and she felt that now was the time to go there. It seemed that Friendship House no longer needed her (perhaps no longer wanted her.) That was very hard to accept. But a Bishop had invited her, and this seemed to be the time to accept that invitation.

They settled their affairs in Chicago and New York, and Eddie resigned his jobs with various newspapers. He too had learned to trust Divine Providence and to lead a simple life based on God's will. They put together their meagre belongings, and loaded a car, which he had purchased with the last of his money, and headed for a way of life different from any they had known previously. It was to be a wonderful and exciting life about which Eddie was to write later: ''I never covered a story more exciting than Madonna House!'' But at that moment he had to be a support to Catherine who was in a state of shock, heartbroken by the rejection of her American children.

Chapter Eleven

SPIRITUAL DIRECTION

Two wonderful friends during her Friendship House days continued to stand by Catherine and to support her. They were Father Paul of Graymoor, founder of the Atonement Fathers of Garrison, New York, and Father Henry Carr of the Basilian Fathers, in Toronto. Here I feel we should say something about the wonderful men who directed Catherine spiritually, and about her own deep appreciation and love for spiritual direction.

Throughout the centuries, spiritual direction has always been considered one of the essential means of acquiring the spirit of Christ. Christians who have desired to follow the Lord, fully and wholeheartedly, have sought out those who were experienced in the ways of God. These people are able to listen carefully to God and to discern in souls what really comes from God, and what may come only from ourselves, or from the devil, who tempts us to do things which can destroy us spiritually. The great St. Bernard of Clairvaux has said: ''He who directs himself becomes the disciple of a fool.''

Catherine was deeply convinced of the need for a spiritual guide. It was part and parcel of her whole attitude to God and to the Church. As a child of twelve in Egypt, she had had a spiritual director. She knew deeply the value of such a relationship, and since she sought God more than anything else, she knew she needed desperately to subject her thoughts, ideas and inspirations to another person. She has written about this and the difficulty she encountered in finding a spiritual director in North America:

One of the great gifts that the Sacrament of the Priesthood confers on humble and ordinary men is the gift of spiritual direction, which today would be translated as a very special, and extraordinary ability to discern the ways of the Holy Spirit in the soul of man.

It is truly a gift of the Lord to the priesthood, and no priest should refuse the request for spiritual direction, because he really doesn't direct... God directs... no priest should refuse to direct any man, woman or child who asks him... The laity are floundering... without direction...

When I first came to North America, I was very much astonished that quite a few priests not exactly refused me spiritual direction when I asked them, but tried to ''get out of it.'' One pleaded humbly that he wasn't an expert in spiritual direction; another said he was too busy. I cannot recall the other excuses.

I was sorely perturbed, for since the age of twelve, I had had a spiritual director, and I was kind of lost without one. So having occasion to talk to a bishop, I asked him what was the matter with the priests of North America that they shied away from directing people. The reply of the bishop astounded me even more than the difficulty with the priests. He said that in this new world the seminaries did not teach mystical theology, and that the best way to find a director was to go to the Religious Orders such as the Carmelites, Franciscans, Dominicans etc.

I cannot understand this very well, because you don't need ''mystical knowledge'' to direct a human soul; you

100

need prayer, and a surrender to the Holy Spirit. You need a realization that *you* are not directing. God is doing it for you by giving you this tremendous gift of discernment from a person with a particular ''grace of state.''

On the other hand, I was astonished also that in the '20s, the '30s and even the '40s, the laity were almost unaware of the need for spiritual direction. I started telling everybody who wanted to listen that they needed a spiritual director if they wanted to follow the narrow way of the Lord.

Finally Catherine was able to find a good priest who was her director for a few years. His name was Father John Milway Filion, and he was the Provincial of the Jesuits in Toronto. He was able to be a good friend and a help to Catherine. Another Jesuit, Father Keating, also directed Catherine for a time.

When Catherine met Father Paul of Graymoor, the founder of the (Franciscan) Atonement Fathers, she was much drawn to him. She sensed that he was truly a man of God. Father Paul Wattson had been an Episcopalian priest, and had decided to join the Catholic Church. The whole purpose of his life was to labor for the reunion of Christendom. He suffered greatly from the terrible divisions between Christians, and worked mightily to bring Catholics and other Christians back together. He founded two religious congregations: the Friars of the Atonement, and the Sisters of the Atonement. He instituted the Church Unity Octave to pray for this unity. It is observed from January 18 to January 25 each year.

Catherine found in Father Paul a wonderful friend, benefactor and protector. When she founded Friendship House in Toronto, he was her principal support. He not only encouraged her; he helped her financially as well, and always gave her good advice. Father Paul remained her loyal friend to the end.

101

Another spiritual guide and good friend to Catherine was Father Henry Carr, C.S.B. In the early days of Friendship House, Toronto, he was the Father General of the Basilian Order, with headquarters at St. Michael's College there. He had founded the Institute for Mediaeval Studies in Toronto, and had accomplished much in the field of higher education for Catholics. He was well known and loved.

Catherine was attracted to him because she saw in him a man who was close to God, a man of prayer, a man of decision, of leadership. She trusted him completely and obeyed him totally. Father Carr was a great influence on Catherine's spiritual life. She always came out of St. Michael's College, after a visit with Father Carr, with fresh enthusiasm — renewed, lighthearted, and unburdened. He was of incredible help to her at the time, and remained her spiritual director until she left Toronto for Harlem.

There was another priest who directed Catherine for some ten years. He was Father Paul Hanly Furfey, head of the Sociology Department at Catholic University in Washington, D.C. Catherine met him when she was invited to lecture there.

It must be said, to his eternal glory, that he healed her of the wounds of Toronto by his total acceptance of her. He had a special charism to lead his directees to the contemplative life, although he was totally unaware of this. God chose him to guide Catherine in that stage of her spiritual life, and he was most faithful to that mission. Assisted by the Holy Spirit he was able to bring her to contemplation, and to the full flowering of the mystical life. For this alone may he be forever glorified!

Some day their whole correspondence should be published. For now, let us quote a few extracts:

Catherine to Fr. Furfey: How different I am from what I could and should be, or what people think I am, and — what is more important — what God would like me to be — a burden that becomes intolerable at times. Will you pray that I may learn to love, love God *really* with my whole heart and soul as he deserves, and should be loved? Dimly I realize that in that love is hidden the whole secret of sanctity, the key of heaven, the reason for my existence, the Alpha and Omega of my life. I desire so much to love him, and I do; but my love seems so small, weak and puny before his loveliness and beauty, before that tremendous drawing power that he has. I have prayed for a spiritual director who would teach me to love God completely, absolutely perfectly. And then I often think: 'But can we poor, finite mortals love like that at all?' And St. Francis looks on my thoughts and smiles, for he, at least, knows that *we can.*

Fr. Furfey to Catherine: Of course you are right in wanting to be a saint. Why should you have any hesitation about that holy ambition? To say that one does not want to be a saint is deliberately to place a limit on one's love for God, and that is always a very serious mistake... It makes me very happy not only that you have this beautiful ambition, but also that you are following it out in a most thoroughly Catholic way. I think that the renunciation that you are practicing, plus the works of mercy, plus, above all things, the liturgy, constitute the simple and natural way of progressing in holiness.

Catherine to Fr. Furfey: I did not realize that I am part and parcel of a new movement, small as yet, but which is bound to leave its impression on the sands of time, and on the history of the Catholic Church... Having faced up to this frightening picture, and, as it were, prostrating myself before God in fear and trembling, yet peacefully and humbly, I come to the next point. If this is so, then the answer is clear: I must do it. In order to do it well, I must throw myself more and more onto God. The first thought that comes to me is PRAYER and ever more PRAYER. I do not mean only oral ones; no, mental, meditation, contemplation even. Yes, Father, imagine: I, who was always afraid of this word, am now willing to embrace it if it is God's will.

Fr. Furfey to Catherine: About contemplation, first of all: We must distinguish between mystical or infused contemplation on the one hand, and ordinary or acquired contemplation on the other. Infused contemplation is an extraordinary gift of God, and there is nothing that we can do of our own efforts to acquire it. This seems to be the species of contemplation you have in mind in your letter. But there is another kind of contemplation, which is not a special gift of God except in the sense that any sort of prayer is a grace. Acquired contemplation means simply thinking about God or holy things in a particular way. What is this 'particular way?' It is not discursive reasoning. It is rather a simple looking at the truth. If you go into Church and simply think, 'There is God; and here am I,' and then you kneel there quietly with your mind fixed on the Divine Presence, not saying any prayer, not reasoning, but merely looking on God with your consciousness occupied with the thought of the Divine Perfection — then that is acquired contemplation, and it is not above the capacities of any moderately serious Catholic.

Later he reminds her that to neglect contemplation is to ''be getting away from the 'soul of the apostolate.' ''

These are some of the wonderful priests whom God sent to Catherine to guide her at various stages of her spiritual journey. They all seemed to have had a special gift to realize that hers was no ordinary soul; that God had special designs on her life, even though the totality of these designs was as yet a mystery.

Later, when she most needed it, God was to send her another priest who would have a very special grace to direct mystics. He was to become, until his death, a most loyal support for Catherine. His name was Father John Callahan, and I will speak of him later on.

Truly Catherine was always blessed by spiritual directors who were themselves great and holy men.

Chapter Twelve

MADONNA HOUSE — A MYSTERY OF GOD'S DESIGN

I have mentioned the rejection Catherine suffered as she left Friendship House in Harlem. Throughout her life she experienced moments of overwhelming rejections. First there was the rejection by Mother Russia after the Revolution of 1917. It is very difficult for Russians to have to accept asylum outside of their own beloved country. They are so rooted in their own faith, in their traditions, lifestyles, their forests, lakes, rivers and immense steppes. They have been intimately united for more than 4,000 years with their own soil, their own physical environment. Rejection of Catherine by Mother Russia made of her an exile — a refugee for life. Much as she has been well received in Canada and the United States, she always felt orphaned, a stranger in many ways.

Then there was the rejection she experienced in Toronto when she felt obliged to leave that city. Now there was added the rejection she felt as she left the United States and headed for Canada. She had been maligned, misunderstood, persecuted. She had suffered great loneliness. She was severely tempted to abandon all of her ideals, even to destroy herself by suicide. She knew all of the temptations, all of the doubts that we can experience. But throughout all of this, her great consolation was the rejected Christ, and she identified with him in his agony; she grew in faith, in hope and in love. She could always empathize deeply with the lonely and the rejected. The anguish of all mankind was *her* anguish too.

God had given her Eddie; and he consoled, supported, and protected her most tenderly. Together, they now had to face a completely new lifestyle. They had to walk in faith into what can only be called a mystery of God's design. Both said repeatedly that they felt they had reached "the end of the road." They felt they would live their last years in this little house by the river, writing books, living by begging, and ministering quietly to a few neighbors. Even though they had a mandate from the Bishop, they felt that, very likely, few people would come to Combermere. But they were both overwhelmingly mistaken!

Toronto had given Catherine to Canada. So much so that the holy and wise Archbishop Michael C. O'Neill of Regina had called her "Catherine of Canada." Harlem had given her to the United States, and made interracial justice famous during the pioneering days of the '40s. She and Dorothy Day had become the center of attraction to all who were interested in the lay apostolate, in social justice, in liturgy, labor unions, and interracial justice. Now Combermere was about to give Catherine to the whole world. She and Eddie and the house they were to found — Madonna House — would affect the whole world in ways which they could never have foreseen, and some of which are yet to be revealed.

Let us talk briefly about Combermere itself — its history and its people. Geographically it is situated in the foothills of the Laurentian mountains, in what is known as the Canadian Shield. It is a land of forest, lakes and rivers, and the area is about a thousand feet above sea level.

This part of Canada was originally opened up by lumber barons. The region became famous for its majestic, white pines which were immense. They were greatly in demand for the building of ships. The British Navy, for instance, prized this white pine highly, and used it for the masts of its mighty fleet. There were other wonderful trees also such as cedar, oak, birch, maple and aspen.

Gradually the lumberjacks who came to work for the lumber barons cleared the land, and built log cabins for themselves. They brought their families and settled down. In those days it took strong men and women of great courage to come to the Ottawa Valley, the Madawaska Valley. But these people had that courage. They formed a civilization which has been an example of great Christian faith, an example of Christian living to the whole of Canada. The Ottawa Valley has been famous for the number of its vocations to the priesthood and to the religious life. They have helped to evangelize not only their own area, but western Canada as well.

By the end of the century, these wonderful people had to face the fact that the primeval forest had been pretty well cut down. By the '30s and '40s even the second growth was gone, and reforestation would not occur for some years. Since this area is not a good agricultural area either, the people who had settled here were having a hard time. They had not shared in the prosperity brought about by World War II, as it was not an industrial area. Combermere and the area around it was considered a pocket of poverty, and Bishop William Smith of Pembroke was happy to have Catherine and Eddie come here to help these stalwart people.

On May 17, 1947, Catherine and Eddie arrived in Combermere. They came to the little six-room house built by a lifelong friend, Nicholas Makletzoff. It was on the bank of the Madawaska right where this beautiful (that's the meaning of the name) river formed a lovely bay.

The scenery was exquisite, but conditions were quite primitive. The nearest doctor and railroad were ten miles away in a little town called Barry's Bay. The roads were rather poor. There was no electricity in the area. Kerosene lamps were used for lighting homes. However, there were telephones here. A bus passed through Combermere on its way from Toronto to Pembroke. Water was pumped from a well in the yard and carried in. Wood was used for heating. The nearest hospital was in Bancroft, 35 miles away. Obviously, life here would be quite a challenge to city folks, but Catherine and Eddie had realized that and were ready to accept it.

Physical hardships were nothing to Catherine next to the inner pain and rejection that she had been through. Here in the quiet, calm, protective woodlands of eastern Ontario, she was gradually to be healed. However, it took a long time before she could meet people without interiorly lifting a protective arm. It was a long time before she could become again her joyful and bouncy self. It took months before she could open the gate, cross the road, and go out visiting, without shaking with the fear of rejection. All of the suffering she had endured had affected her heart, but she did not give in; she plunged into the work of settling in.

It is wonderful to note that Grace Flewelling (better known as "Flewy"), who had been with Catherine at Friendship House, and who came soon after Catherine and Eddie, remained loyal to Catherine until her (Flewy's) death in 1951. She was the right arm of

Catherine in everything, and is venerated by the staff as a remarkable woman and one of the great pioneers of Friendship House and Madonna House.

The three of them worked mightily that summer, making a home of the little house, establishing a garden in the poor soil, obtaining some hens and pigs and caring for them. Donations at that time were few and far between, and they lived most poorly. They had to pump and carry water, cook on the wood stove, and endure the hardships of pioneers anywhere. It was not easy, but it was a challenge, and they had each other.

However, not very long after their arrival, Eddie suffered a serious heart attack, and from that time on was unable to help in the physical part of the work. He had been a star reporter, and was a clever writer, so he spent much of his time writing books. These helped the financial situation to some extent, and certainly made him feel he was contributing to the house even though he could not engage in physical activity. Eddie spent most of his life in Madonna House writing, and being a loving, supportive presence to everybody who came. He never complained about the pain or discomfort he suffered. He spent a lot of time in bed at various times, and staffworkers would often visit him for comfort and strength.

In the first years, much discussion took place among various bishops and priests about what Madonna House should be and do in the diocese. But Catherine, in her own heart, had always known that the best thing to do is to listen to God; to respond to the needs of people in simple and humble ways without a lot of equipment or expenditures of money. She was always adamant about begging and depending upon the providence of God. She believed in going to a city or a town, finding a house, making it habitable, and living there. She believed in praying, visiting people, listening to them, and receiving them as they came. In this way a wonderful apostolate would develop out of the needs as you learned about them.

This is how the work in Combermere developed. Catherine saw the need for books to read, and formed a service of lending them by mail to isolated areas. She begged for clothing, medical supplies, and various household needs. She and Flewy spent hours on what she called the "chit-chat" apostolate, getting to know the neighbors and the needs of the area. The Madonna House Apostolate began without plans, programs or blueprints. But the Holy Spirit clearly showed the way.

Some were suspicious of Catherine and her work for a few years, especially those who were not Catholic. But the Lord took care of that in a wonderful way. People found out that Catherine was a nurse, and since there was no hospital or doctor in Combermere, Catherine was often called upon to visit the sick, to deliver a baby, or to attend an accident. A whole book could be written about her experiences as "bush nurse." She became known and loved by the people whom she served so faithfully, and they gradually came to trust her, even those who might have been most prejudiced against a "popish, religious woman."

It is a miracle of God's grace that even though she went out in all kinds of weather, she never suffered an accident, never got stuck anywhere, and no matter what the weather was, she never failed to get through and return home safely. No matter how tired she was, she never refused a nursing call, and she never let herself be affected in the least by bigotry. She was hardly aware of it.

One day in the summer of 1947, another child of the Apostolate of Madonna House was born. It was to link Madonna House with the whole world.

It happened this way. Catherine and Eddie were

112

sitting before the fireplace in the main room of their little cottage. Suddenly Catherine said: "Let us start a newspaper, and call it *Restoration*!" Eddie jumped at the idea. Newspaperman to the core, he was thrilled with the idea of having his own newspaper and editing it for Catherine. The name would symbolize their idea of restoring the whole world to Christ. The little paper would be well named.

The first issue of *Restoration* appeared in December, 1947. In it Catherine outlined its purpose. Eddie was its editor, Catherine its managing editor, and Grace Flewelling, staff artist. In it Catherine begged for clothing, medicines, and books for the people whom she served. It was a small paper, with "infinite ideas," as Catherine was to describe it. (*Restoration*, at the present writing, has a circulation of around 10,000, and it pretty well circles the entire world.)

To Catherine and Eddie's great surprise, volunteers came to live the life of Madonna House for awhile, and to help in the good work they were doing. Catherine received them all and proceeded to train them with great patience. She trained "on the job." But she also believed in their taking courses of all kinds: farming, bookkeeping, weaving, dairying, cheesemaking and so on. She felt that nothing that could further the kingdom of God was alien to the Apostolate.

Catherine always loved to teach, and lunch time was her favorite teaching period. She spoke extensively about God and the things of God, the Apostolate, the needs of the world, the needs of the people. Her talks were clear, full of wisdom and deep human and spiritual insights.

The financial needs became greater as more people came, and Catherine continued to beg more and more and to trust in God to provide. He always did, but often Madonna House was overdrawn at the bank.

She operated in the red until after Vatican II when Madonna House became better known. She was happy to do so, for this meant a total trust in God. She was much happier when she was short of money than she was in later years when donations began to pour in. She always took her financial needs to the Infant of Prague, to Jesus Christ as a Child, and somehow enough always came through when it was most needed, or the overdraft was as its greatest.

Priests and others wondered what *was* this life going on at Madonna House? Was it really a vocation? Was it from God? Was it simply one woman's illusion? Was Catherine Doherty keeping people from accepted forms of religious life? This appeared to be a raggedy type of community. They went barefoot. They wore poor clothing. They were men and women living together. Parents were often furious when their children joined this community. Many stories circulated about this strange group in Combermere. Some said that Catherine was a saint; others that she was a devil. She accepted all of this with joy, saying that she was very lucky, because this would help her up the ladder of sanctity. She prayed for her persecutors, even though she could be deeply hurt as anyone of us can. But she always forgave, saying that forgiveness is part and parcel of daily life.

Bishop Smith of Pembroke admired Catherine and Eddie very much. He was never very disturbed by people's reports. He always followed the principle that if it was of God, it would go on, and if it was not, it would take care of itself. He had faith in Catherine and Eddie and heard of all the good they were doing in Combermere. But once he was heard to remark facetiously: ''I live between the nuclear plant to the west of me at Chalk River, and the Baroness to the east of me in Combermere, and I never know which is going to explode first!'' Later, in 1960, he gave Madonna House his official approval. But, before this, it had been for Catherine, Eddie, Grace Flewelling, and all of the others whose lives have made Madonna House possible, a walk in great faith in the mystery of God's design.

Chapter Thirteen

1951 — A YEAR OF GRACE

At the beginning of the new year of 1951 Catherine had not the slighest idea of what her Apostolate would become, or if it would continue at all. She lived one day at a time, never concerned about the morrow. She never doubted that God would provide for all of the needs of the Apostolate, if it was meant to continue. She felt sure that God would reveal to her what he wanted Madonna House to be and to do. She lived totally free, totally abandoned to his will. She nestled in his arms like a child. I have always been awed by her childlike faith and total trust in God; by her total confidence in Our Lady. I saw this no matter what accusations were leveled against her, and no matter what suffering and pain life brought to her. She simply said: ''God is my joy. God is my strength.''

She had regained her health, and was now very strong physically, psychologically and spiritually. She had become again a mighty instrument of God's love and mercy; of his justice also. Many came to talk to her, and her volunteers loved her.

1951 appears to me as a year when God manifested his great tenderness for Catherine in rather extraordinary ways. The first thing that stands out in my mind is that he sent her four people who were to become the cornerstones of a stable Madonna House Apostolate. Others had come and gone since 1947, but these four were to remain.

They were Dorothy Phillips, Louie Stoeckle, Marie Thérèse Langlois and Mamie Legris. They were four large stones upon which to build a house. Their loyalty, dedication and perseverance have been an example to all. They were pioneers in the true sense of the word. Catherine spent hours training and indoctrinating them, and just being with them. They became dependable, prayerful people who persevered under very great difficulties.

The coming of Mamie Legris, who was a native of the Ottawa valley and a respected teacher, had a great influence upon the local priests and people. Mamie had a good reputation and, at that time, Madonna House did not. It was not understood. One lady was known to remark: ''Well, Madonna House can't be all bad, because Mamie Legris has joined it!'' Catherine always appreciated Mamie's loyalty, devotion and perseverance, and looked upon her as a true friend.

The next great gift came about in a most simple and unforeseen manner. In 1950, Catherine was preparing for the Summer School which Madonna House offered yearly. Young people came for a week or more to learn about social justice, the Mass, Our Lady, or the lay apostolate. Generally, Catherine tried to get a priest to give a lecture each week. This particular year the thought came to her to invite her good friend, Father Eugene Cullinane, a Basilian priest. Perhaps he would be willing to come.

Father Gene, as he was called, had three great loves: Our Lady, social justice and the lay apostolate. Political economy was his specialty, and he had taught at a number of universities. He was an expert on the social justice of the Church, and a holy man. At this time he was president of Aquinas Institute in Rochester, New York. There he had met Father John Thomas Callahan, a diocesan priest, who was also immensely interested in the lay apostolate, and a great lover of Our Lady. They found they had much in common, and became good friends.

When Father Cullinane received Catherine's invitation to Summer School, he was unable to go because of previous commitments. Suddenly, he got an idea: why not ask Father John Callahan? Perhaps he would be willing to go to Madonna House. Father Callahan said, ''Yes, I'll go,'' little realizing that those three little words would determine the most important decision of his life.

Father John Callahan was in his late thirties, and had been ordained for twelve years. He was greatly involved in the lay apostolate. He ran six radio programs a week, was director of the Council of Catholic Women, chaplain at Mercy High School, and founder of various apostolic groups in Rochester, New York. He was also very interested in social justice, and had written a couple of pamphlets on the social encyclicals.

When Father Callahan arrived at Madonna House, Catherine saw a handsome, tall, energetic, and holy priest. She sensed his holiness, and was immediately attracted to him in her spirit.

In 1951, when Catherine asked Father Callahan to be her spiritual director, he hesitated, saying he would pray about it. In later years he told me why he had hesitated to accept Catherine as a directee. It was not that he felt inferior to the job. It was because he knew that she was a foundress, and that in directing her he would be involved in the life and direction of a whole spiritual family. That was what made him take time to pray and think about it for so long.

God had given Father Callahan good preparation to be a spiritual director. As a seminarian, he had been attracted to what is known as spiritual theology, such as the works of St. John of the Cross, St. Francis de Sales, St. Teresa of Avila, as well as the writings of other great mystics. His own clear mind and clean heart readily absorbed the events he read about, the principles involved, the magnificent experiences which these saints had undergone through the influence of the Holy Spirit. Father Callahan truly had the charism of spiritual direction.

Later he was to direct, not only Catherine, but most of the early members of the Apostolate and many others. He was to have an extraordinary career as a spiritual director, and to form all of the priests in Madonna House to be good spiritual directors. Through his influence and his very person, spiritual direction was to become an essential element of the Madonna House way of life, and one of its greatest contributions. He was to have an immense influence upon the whole Apostolate.

I have said that 1951 was a year of grace, but it also brought sadness. Grace Flewelling, who had been Catherine's constant companion since the very beginnings of Friendship House in Toronto, passed to her eternal reward on August 8. She had suddenly experienced chest pains which proved to be serious. A priest happened to be visiting Madonna House and gave her the last Sacraments. Catherine was with her when she died. It was a sad loss for her, but she offered Flewy to God, and set about the duty of the moment. She rejoiced that her beloved friend had persevered to the end, and often used her as a shining example of humble, persevering service, of good humor amidst trials, of patience, and a total lack of self-centeredness. She had worked hard and served God well.

The death of Flewy turned out to be a gracious gift of God, as well as a sorrow. The volunteers who were present at Madonna House at the time began to think seriously of replacing her. They began to think of giving themselves to this kind of vocation, even if it was unusual and new in the Church. After Flewy's death, people began to join Madonna House, and the Apostolate was launched.

The lay apostolate had grown and developed in the Church since the early 1900's. Pius X had told his cardinals that the greatest need of the Church was devoted laymen and women. The Popes had greatly encouraged the development of lay groups, and the training of lay people to be apostles. Some fifty groups, in various countries, unknown to each other, had developed in the Church over the years. Many were living in poverty, chastity and obedience.

Pius XII, a man of vision and understanding, felt that the time had come to hold an International Congress of the Lay Apostolate in Rome. His announcement of this was received with mixed feelings in the Catholic world. There was great jubilation among the people involved in the lay apostolate. For so many years they had been suspect and misunderstood in the Church. Now they were being recognized by the very Father of Christendom. They were being called together to exchange experiences, and to elaborate programs. Some received this announcement with fear. What would now happen in the Church? Would this threaten the work of priests and bishops? Would the Church be subject to a mighty wave of anticlericalism?

Catherine was delighted with this announcement. The mere fact that this Congress was to be held filled her heart with a joy she had never quite known. Some twenty years ago she had given her whole self to the lay apostolate. She had done this in pure faith. At that time she had been told by Archbishop Neil McNeil that she was fifty years ahead of her time. He had recognized a special movement of the Holy Spirit in her, and felt it was the beginnings of the lay apostolate in the Church. Now the Pope himself was calling this Congress of the Lay Apostolate.

Catherine rejoiced immensely and thanked God. She rejoiced, not only for herself, not only that her own intuitions had been finally proven true. She rejoiced that the Church, the Beautiful Bride of Christ, the people of God, and all mankind would benefit from this meeting of the laity under the paternal guidance, friendship, and blessing of the Holy Father.

Bishop Smith of Pembroke was happy to have Catherine go as a delegate from his diocese, and she was happy to be among the three thousand or so delegates who came to Rome from all over the world. These people, representing a hundred or more nations, were apostles who had suffered much. They were men and women of great faith who were giving themselves to the service of all mankind, irrespective of race, creed, or social status. They had been tried in the fire of persecution and misunderstanding, as Catherine herself had been.

During the Congress Catherine was called by Monsignor Giovanni Battista Montini, Substitute Secretary of State. After the Pope, he was the most important man in the Vatican. She immediately began to wonder what was wrong. Maybe this would be the end of her Apostolate. She tried to think of what she had done that the Secretary of State might wish to chastise her for.

She recalled that the day before she had spoken very strongly against the injustices of capitalism. She had spoken in favor of the workingman. In her usual manner, with great sorrow, she had bemoaned the fact that the beautiful, majestic and healing social doctrine of the Church was being ignored by most bishops, priests and lay people all over the world. She thought to herself: "The Secretary of State has heard about this, and he must want to warn me."

When Catherine was ushered into the presence of this gray-haired, middle-aged man of slight stature, she was deeply impressed with his benignity. He greeted her warmly, and she read complete kindness in his eyes. He rose and walked over to greet her. He told her how happy he was to meet her. Catherine sat down, wondering if this was some kind of Roman trick! Was this the kindness before the "kill," like the giving of a good meal before execution?

But she felt more at ease when Monsignor Giovanni said to her: "I am very happy to meet you. I have heard much about your wonderful work in Canada, and your work with the Blacks in the United States. I know of your work in interracial justice and in social justice. I want you to know that the Holy Father is pleased with you."

At this moment Catherine responded by passing out! When she came to, there was this smiling dignitary bending over her, and putting a glass of wine to her lips. He said, "Drink this; you'll feel better." Then he continued: "You may wonder why I have called you."

He traced the work of the Holy Spirit throughout the Church down through the ages: the growth of monasticism, the Fathers of the Desert, the contemplative orders, the mendicant orders, and the active congregations. He pointed out how the Holy Spirit had always provided for the needs of the times by inspiring these founders and foundresses.

He pointed out that, since 1900, the Holy Spirit's special concern seems to be that lay people once again find their place in the world. He said that there were already in existence about a hundred groups of lay-men, laywomen, and diocesan priests who wished to consecrate themselves to the service of God in a very special way. He called these groups Secular Institutes. He said that in 1947 they were recognized by Pope Pius XII as a work of the Holy Spirit, and he had given them a charter called *Provida Mater Ecclesiæ*. These people could make a permanent commitment under vows, oaths, or promises. They could have a legal status in the Church, even though at that time they were not actually mentioned in the Code of Canon Law.

Monsignor Giovanni Montini then said: ''The Holy Father and I would like you to consider this new development in the Church. You and your followers have been in existence now for some twenty years. We would like you to pray and sincerely ponder whether or not you should write a definite Constitution and ask your followers to commit themselves, not just for an indiscriminate number of months or years, but for life. We would like to see you become a permanent, stable, spiritual family in the Church.''

He smiled a wonderful smile and said: ''I know that you would love to see the Holy Father. I have arranged a private interview; it will take place tomorrow at ten o'clock.''

The interview was over. Catherine rose from her seat, knelt for his blessing, kissed his hand, wetting it with her tears, said ''Thank you,'' and walked away. She was floating on cloud nine, wondering if this was real or a fantasy of her own extremely creative imagination!

She had sought to live hidden and unknown, praying, fasting and giving alms. She had wanted only to please the Father and to give joy to her brothers and sisters. All of this approval, this consolation, the fact that the Pope had called together the lay apostolate and recognized its place in the Church, the fact that Monsignor Montini wanted her and her family to have a legal status in the Church — all of this was just too much to absorb! All she could do was to praise God, thank him, and wonder what the future would hold.

Catherine arrived at the Vatican next morning properly dressed in the black dress and veil which was appropriate for an interview with the Holy Father. She was brought into a room, and stood there waiting.

Within minutes a tall, luminous figure dressed in white walked rapidly towards her. It was Pope Pius XII. She knelt and kissed his ring. The Holy Father took her hands and raised her from her knees. He looked at her intently and said, "Madame has suffered much." Catherine's eyes filled with tears she could not restrain. "Persevere, persevere, persevere," he said. Then he added, "The world is headed for very difficult times. The fate of the Church, and of our own person depends upon people like you and institutes like yours. Persevere."

They spoke a little more, and he told her to always support Catholic families because they have such a burden to carry in this world. Then he was wafted away to the next pressing duty of the moment.

Catherine was delighted beyond words; she was dazed. At last she had met the Pope, the Vicar of Christ, whom she had loved and honored all of her life. She had always been as faithful as the Northern Star to the hierarchy of the Church. She was laying down her life for that Church.

Eddie was in Rome obtaining material for a book. Soon after the interview they met in a restaurant to discuss everything. Catherine was radiant from her encounter with the Holy Father. As they sipped some good Roman wine both realized the price that they would have to pay to become a stable, religious family under vows. If Madonna House decided to follow the instructions of Monsignor Montini, not only would they continue to live in poverty and obedience; they would be *celibate* as well! Hard as it might be, they already accepted this possibility with joyful hearts.

Upon her return, Catherine told all about the interviews and the wishes of the Holy Father. The staff knew little of the legalities of ''canonical status,'' but many of them wanted the permanency of a lifelong dedication. They felt called to that. So, promises of poverty, chastity and obedience were taken. They were happy that Rome had spoken, and Madonna House had been recognized as a great work of the Holy Spirit, and invited into the Church by the Holy Father himself, speaking personally to Catherine.

Indeed, 1951 had been a year of great grace!

Chapter Fourteen

MYSTICISM

For some years now, Catherine had labored strenuously to acquire every virtue. She had prayed and fasted in a most extraordinary way. Father Furfey, her spiritual director before she had left the United States in 1947, recognized that God was developing in her the gift of contemplation. She was entering a totally new state of the spiritual life. He advised her to get another spiritual director because he did not feel at ease with the contemplative life.

It may appear strange to some that spiritual direction should be needed by anyone who is becoming so closely united to God. We need spiritual direction at all times in our lives, and when a person reaches the higher stages of the spiritual life, direction is not only needed, it is essential. As a person grows closer to God, the light of His presence is blinding to the spirit. This is so true that people think they are walking in total darkness, not knowing where they are going.

In the early stages of the spiritual life, Catherine had striven mightily to become holy — to please God in all things. In a previous chapter I gave some excerpts from her writings about these struggles. Her diaries are absolutely magnificent concerning the deeper aspects of her life with God, and some day these may be more accessible.

Now the wind of the Holy Spirit began to take over, and her soul became as a little boat which has just acquired a lovely, broad sail. She was being moved in many directions without effort. This confused her; she was accustomed to hard, ascetical labor. It was precisely at this point that Catherine needed a new spiritual guide.

God always provides, and she believed that with all of her soul. It had always been true for every single thing in her life, and he would not fail her now. God *was* to provide a sure guide for her in a most mysterious and delightful way. It was not at all the way that any of us would have chosen.

It was now early in the year 1952, and Father John Callahan had accepted to be Catherine's spiritual director. She had invited him to give the yearly retreat to the staff in April, and he had accepted. He was at Madonna House when suddenly he collapsed from exhaustion. Catherine called a doctor, and he prescribed a total rest for some time. Catherine put Fr. Callahan in one of the little cabins and nursed him. It was a good time for long talks and getting to know one another.

One day, as Father Callahan rested on a lawn chair in the sun, a deep conviction came to him: "This is my second vocation. The lay apostolate needs priests. I shall become the chaplain of this group." He was thoroughly convinced that God wanted him to be not only Catherine's spiritual director, but also the chaplain for this struggling, little group of lay apostles.

Eddie Doherty told me one day that the coming of Father Callahan to the Apostolate was like the electricity being turned on. He said: "Madonna House had finally found its soul."

Catherine was delighted. She was most grateful to have such a good spiritual director, and she thanked God who had sent a priest to the Apostolate. Never in her wildest imagination had she thought that priests would join her and become part and parcel of her apostolic family. Father Callahan's clear decision filled her with unspeakable joy.

The great gift that Father Callahan was to Catherine at this time will be known only when more of the depths of her mystical life are revealed. As a spiritual director, he was most at home with mystics. In him they found understanding, detachment and assurance. He was a past master in the ways of mysticism. Where most priests would have sought help somewhere, Father Callahan never hesitated. He knew the ways of God, and with mystics was a giant among men. His discernment was incredibly clear, sincere and beautiful.

God gave Father Callahan to Catherine at a moment when she was being led by God along a mysterious and difficult path of mysticism. In his book, *The Ascent of Mount Carmel*, St. John of the Cross writes of this state:

> On a dark night, Kindled in love with yearnings — oh, happy chance!
> I went forth without being observed, My house being now at rest.

No one is more grateful to a spiritual director than a mystic, since no one is more confused and lost. The mystic falls into the hands of the living God — into a veritable Fire. The Holy Spirit moves the soul as a leaf is moved by the wind. A spiritual director who understands brings light, direction, clarity, and relief to the mystic. He helps the directee to fight off illusions and the incredibly strong attacks of the Evil One.

Catherine had a deep relationship with God. She was always afraid that more of her mystical life would become known to others. She, who had always talked about finding God in the ordinary things of everyday life, wanted to keep this other part of her life a "secret of the King." But one phenomenon was often witnessed by the staff and others who were at Mass with us. However, most did not fully understand what was taking place.

Catherine frequently experienced the gift of ecstasy. Often, after Holy Communion, she would be leaning on the bench in front of her, and suddenly she would faint. It happened in a second, and it lasted a few minutes. Then she would come to, kneel, or stand again if the liturgy required it, as if nothing had happened.

People would rush to open a window, and visitors wanted to do more; but they were told to just leave her alone. Catherine herself would pass it off as a fainting spell, and many believed that it was only that.

It was ecstasy, wherein all the senses are suspended, and all the faculties are held by the Holy Spirit who descends suddenly upon a person, He plunges, like a bird of prey, grabs the person and carries her into another world. In the theology books this is known as "raptus." There she would live for a few moments in the intense joy of heaven, of the Trinity, of her great lover, the Lord Jesus Christ.

The great mystics have known this experience. St. Paul speaks of it (2 Cor 12): "I know a man in Christ who, fourteen years ago was caught up — whether still in the body or out of the body, I do not know, God knows — was caught up into paradise and heard things which must not and cannot be put into human language."

To be a mystic means to be totally free, but under obedience. The charism of a mystic's spiritual director is to recognize the freedom the directee has been called upon to exercise, but to set up the signposts and the safeguards. Father Callahan knew well how to do this. Under his capable direction, Catherine forayed into the night, without hesitation. God, in his great mercy, had sent her the guide she needed, to walk with assurance under the stars.

Chapter Fifteen

THE APOSTOLATE GROWS

1954 had been declared a Marian Year by Pope Pius XII. We felt at the time that to have a year dedicated to Our Lady was significant for each one of us. It marked a year of special intercession. At Madonna House it was observed with great joy by both staff and visitors.

In the fall of 1953 Bishop Jean Louis Coudert visited Madonna House. He was an Oblate of Mary Immaculate, and a great missionary bishop. Catherine always called him "the last of the great giants of the North." I think it was Parkman, the great American historian, who called the Oblate missionary the greatest man produced by the 19th century. Why had Bishop Coudert come to Madonna House?

One often wonders just how did he hear about it, and why did he have such trust in Catherine and this little group of lay apostles. There were six staff workers at the time and six applicants. But Bishop Coudert was a man of wisdom — a man moved by the Holy Spirit — and he trusted the movement of that Spirit enough to ask for a Madonna House mission house in Whitehorse, his diocesan seat.

He asked Catherine for a house which would be a

home for all of the Indian people of the Yukon who had to come into Whitehorse for various purposes. It would also be a refuge for men and women who were without funds, and needed a place to stay for a few days or weeks. It would be a place where the whites and Indians could meet as brothers and sisters.

Catherine did not refuse; she discussed the possibility. Later she flew to Whitehorse. Whitehorse was like an island, a world away from the world, a satellite where little she saw corresponded to other places. On the human level, nothing could possibly have attracted Catherine to live in the Yukon, or send any of her staff there.

Then one morning she had a vision, literally a visual vision, of Our Lady of the Yukon. As Catherine was leaving the convent where she was staying, she saw an Indian lady standing on the street. She was dressed in a white parka which covered her from head to toe. She carried an infant in her arms.

When Catherine told Bishop Coudert about the lady she had seen and how she was dressed, he said, "That kind of parka disappeared years ago. It is just non-existent at the present time." Catherine never made a great deal of the incident. She never said, "I had a vision of Our Lady." But what else can one conclude?

Catherine did love the Indian people, and there had been this lady whose presence seemed a confirmation of the Bishop's request, so she accepted the invitation of Bishop Coudert. In 1954 she sent Mamie Legris, Kathleen O'Herin, and Louie Stoeckle to Whitehorse to open the mission they called "Maryhouse." This humble beginning was to be the first of many houses which were to be founded later in other parts of the world.

By 1957, the Apostolate was really growing. Father Gene Cullinane had told Catherine, in 1956, that he was praying for eighteen staff workers to come within a year's time. His prayers were being answered. Men and women who were seriously interested in joining Madonna House came as volunteers. They desired to live among us for awhile and share our lives. More and more guests came to stay a few days with us.

Catherine always felt that the guests should share in our prayer and in our work. She felt it could be as fruitful as a retreat, to live the humble life of Madonna House and experience manual work along with us. She strongly believed in the Benedictine motto: ''Ora et Labora.'' She was following the great tradition of Western monasticism. She was also completely in line with the great tradition of the Desert Fathers, and the monks of the Eastern Church.

When people who came to Madonna House complained there wasn't enough time for prayer, Catherine would say: ''Learn to pray always. Jesus wants us to pray always. It is good to have special moments for prayer, quiet times to recollect ourselves, and we have a minimum of that. There is meditation every morning, spiritual reading, time for private prayer. But I want you to be aware of God in your own heart, and offer everything to him, serving him through the humble service of one another.'' She taught people to make the duty of every moment a prayer.

Catherine had a very happy disposition, but she also suffered upon seeing the pain of Christ in others. I have never met anyone so conscious of the pain of Christ, a pain which she never disassociated from the suffering of her neighbor. She felt this pain deeply in her own mind, heart and spirit. She desired to console her Beloved as she beheld him in suffering humanity.

She would often return from a lecture tour, shaken to the roots of her spirit by all the sorrows she had witnessed: the hunger for God, the loneliness of Christ knocking at so many doors, the indifference of the multitudes. When she returned, she would speak to the staff and guests about what she had seen. She would shout at the top of her voice about the pain of Christ, and how we must all console him. "We must love him with all of our hearts, for *he* is the man who has fallen among robbers. We must be the Good Samaritans; we must give him the oil of our love and the balm of our service."

Thus it was that staff, guests and volunteers were trained constantly to see Christ everywhere and in all tasks, no matter how humble. They learned how to make everything a prayer. As Madonna House grew, Catherine found more ways of training. One of her great joys was building up the world of Madonna House. She set up various departments and trained the heads of these departments in the proper spirit of our little mandate.

In 1957 a farm was purchased. It became a place to grow much of our food, to have some animals, and to train men to work on the soil. Catherine worked closely with the men's department in developing the farm. She saw to it that the men were trained in dairying, maintenance, heating, electricity, plumbing and various other areas. She sent people for courses and brought in films. Some went to Guelph Agricultural College. It was a great joy for her to help set up the farm. Her whole being expanded in teaching us how to cherish the land and make it fruitful.

Catherine loved to sit with her staff in the evening, sharing her knowledge, and talking on whatever subject might arise. She loved being with and training her staff. She often taught them by working along with them on various projects such as sorting and cleaning and cooking. She taught them that everything we do is a prayer. Once she remarked: "I never forget — that is the essence of my joy and enthusiasm — that everything I do, or you do, will eventually lead souls to Christ. This happens while we are doing the duty of the moment joyfully, enthusiastically, and lovingly. For already God accepts that for other souls.''

She taught her staff to love the Mass. She always said that she lived her life between two Masses and that anything could be endured between two Masses. Often in her teachings she would say things like this:

> I find joy in prayer, especially the Mass. My joy is complete during Mass because I AM IN COMMUNION WITH GOD AND ONE WITH HIM. The incredible joy of God coming to us and of worshipping his Father with us, and giving himself to us as food. I cannot describe this.

> I have been a wife twice, and marriage is a good state; but were I asked if it is the supreme state of loving, I would answer, 'NO!' It is a pale reflection of the unity and love, of the oneness that a human being can have with God at Mass and Communion. Nothing equals that.

> To receive him in Holy Communion is the same as having your lover take you in his arms. He is my lover truly. He enfolds me in his arms, and I put my tired head upon his heart. He consoles me with gentleness and tenderness. He gives me courage to go on. He is the Divine Lover.

No one could speak of the growth of the Madonna House Apostolate without mentioning Eddie who with Catherine founded Madonna House, and was one of its most beloved members for so many years.

He was not in the least way involved in its direction, but he was the power of love among us. His room was truly a ''Friendship House,'' a special room of Madonna House, a place of hospitality. Because he had a bad heart condition, he could not do physical work.

But he had been America's great newspaperman; and after he gave up that exciting life to embrace poverty with Catherine, he still continued to write books. Most of his days were spent writing, planning the next book, going for a walk, or playing endless games of Solitaire. And praying! He recited twelve Rosaries a day.

During the evenings many of the staff, the women especially, would come to see Eddie for a little visit, to talk over something and receive consolation, or perhaps just to feel the love, friendship and concern of a truly good man. He was a father to them all. Catherine would often come to discuss the Apostolate, or the outlines for the departments which she was writing, or her concerns of the day. Eddie would listen; he would be entirely present to her problems; but he never interfered with anything. Later, some of the priests would come in, have a word or two with Eddie, then perhaps watch TV with him for awhile. Everyone seemed to gravitate to Eddie's room; he was a big brother or father figure to us all.

Eddie suffered very much during the twenty-eight years he spent at Madonna House. Often he had to just lie in bed quietly because he had such pressure in his heart. But he never complained. He would say, "God wants this for some reason." Through his suffering, through his books, through just being who he was, Eddie brought many people to God. And he brought great consolation to Catherine and to us all.

Shortly after the staff took promises of poverty, chastity and obedience, Catherine and Eddie took them also. They made their promises quietly, in the presence of their spiritual director.[1] This meant living in celibacy for the rest of their lives. Both found this very

---

1. October 30, 1955, in the presence of Father Callahan and Father Cullinane.

difficult, but they lifted it up to God. Those of us who lived with them can truthfully say that there was never for a moment any selfishness manifested by either of them, seeking a consolation or support that could have rightfully been theirs. I can witness to the fact that they both remained faithful to their promises to the end.

Catherine moved to the little cabin on the Island near Madonna House and lived there until she died. Father Eddie had the large room upstairs in Madonna House — the room where so many came to visit. Their example of celibate love made a lasting impression on every person they met. It came at a time when the Church needed such a witness, and it was a light to many, showing that chastity was possible. It was a great strength to the staff of Madonna House in living out their own promise of chastity.

Eddie Doherty, who was such a hidden, quiet part of the growth of the Apostolate, died on May 4, 1975, in the little hospital in Renfrew, Ontario. I had offered Mass by his bedside about eight hours before. He, being a priest by that time, had joined me in the words of consecration. At 10:34 a.m. he quietly fell asleep in the Lord. His doctor, Alex Mickus, and Clare Becker, a staff worker nurse, were with him. Catherine and I were at a nearby motel. Notified, I immediately offered the first mass of the Resurrection at his bedside.

But Catherine and Eddie had together witnessed the fact that under the mantle of their immense, celibate love for many years, a large family had grown up, and it was called Madonna House. Eddie used to say: ''We took a vow of celibacy, and the Lord gave us a hundred children!''

Chapter Sixteen

OUR LADY OF COMBERMERE

When I arrived at Madonna House in the fall of 1955, the overall impression that moved me very deeply was the sense of a special presence of God. And there were two other manifestations which struck me forcefully. The first was an equally strong sense of the presence of Our Lady, the Mother of God. The second was Catherine and Eddie's vow of celibacy that I have just spoken about — a most unusual thing in the history of the Church. Here I would like to say something of Catherine's relationship to the Mother of God, and its consequent effects upon all the members of our family of Madonna House.

Catherine, being Russian, was brought up in the attitudes and beliefs of the Eastern Church. In the East, devotion to Our Lady has never been separated from the fullness of the worship of God: Our Lady is part of the whole faith. She does not, in any way, exist in some separate sphere of her own. She is rarely, if ever, portrayed without the Child in her arms. She is mentioned in the Liturgy immediately after the Consecration. Her feasts are always celebrated with special liturgical prayers within the Eucharist. Always and forever she is praised, honored, beloved, and respected because she is the Mother of God.

Catherine never "developed" a devotion to Our Lady, the Bogoroditza (the one who gave birth to God), as the Russians call her. Mary was part of Catherine's atmosphere as she grew up, and thus part of her very life. She believed in the Mother of God. She loved Our Lady and prayed to her as simply as one breathes the air.

Russians are in the habit of praying to Our Lady of the place where they live. So, when Catherine came to Combermere, she began to pray to Our Lady as "Our Lady of Combermere." She would ask Our Lady of Combermere to help her in her nursing, to send some good staff workers, for clothing, for money and so on. The staff also began to pray to Mary under that title, and soon our visitors also.

One visitor painted a picture of Our Lady of Combermere as she visualized her. It was of Mary standing there with immense rays coming forth from her hands, symbolizing the many graces which were pouring upon the people who were praying with great faith to her. Father Gene found an old German prayer which was translated into English, and became known as the *Prayer to Our Lady of Combermere.* Here it is:

O Mary, you desire so much to see Jesus loved! Since you love me, this is the favor which I ask of you — to obtain for me a great, personal love of Jesus Christ. You obtain from your Son whatever you please. Pray then for me... that I may never lose the grace of God... that I may increase in holiness and perfection from day to day... and that I may faithfully and nobly fulfill the great calling in life which your Divine Son has given me. By that grief which you suffered on Calvary when you beheld Jesus expire on the cross, obtain for me a happy death, that by loving Jesus and you, my Mother, on earth I may receive the reward of loving and blessing you eternally in heaven. Amen.

Gradually, people began to say this little prayer and to love it.

One afternoon, just before supper, Eddie and Catherine had gone for a swim in the Madawaska River, which forms a bay about thirty feet from Madonna House. As they came out of the water, Catherine happened to look to the left. As she did so, she saw the outline of Our Lady amidst the pine trees which were about forty feet away. Eddie also saw this outline of Mary. Today, a statue of Our Lady of Combermere stands exactly on that spot. Few people know this story. Devotion to Mary as Our Lady of Combermere grew because people prayed to her under this title, and received many answers to their prayers. The blessing and erection of the statue of Our Lady of Combermere was a very special privilege for Madonna House at a time when Mary's help and protection was to be especially needed.

After the sessions of the Second Vatican Council there was a real revolution all over the Catholic world. This revolution is understandable. The Church was never more governed by law as during the period from 1918 (the year of the promulgation of the Code of Canon Law), until 1962, the opening of Vatican II. It is interesting that this upheaval was perhaps the strongest among religious Sisters. It is not surprising, because they were, of all Catholics, the most strictly and rigorously regulated.

Many nuns came to see the Madonna House community, to talk to Catherine, or to our priests. Many were rebellious, angry and disturbed. They were questioning their lifestyle, their vocation, the essence of what they should be. Some have still not found their real place as religious women in the Church.

For priests, the struggle was, perhaps, even more painful. They were wounded deeply in their faith. Confronted by so many contradictory opinions concerning the essential mysteries of Christianity, thousands of priests were shaken in their faith. They felt they no longer had any sure answers to moral problems, and all experienced, in one way or another, the searing fires of a multitude of doubts. Many of these priests found their way to Madonna House. Many wished to speak to Catherine, and they found new strength in doing so.

Many young people also came to Madonna House in the early '60s to discuss not only the ethical aspects of the Christian life but the very fundamental truths of faith. Some were even questioning such beliefs as the resurrection of Our Lord Jesus Christ. Later, many of these same youths were to return, hungry for God, and searching to know more about relating to him in prayer. Our Lady of Combermere had touched them, and they were changed.

Throughout all of these years which were so difficult for the Church and for the world, Catherine remained unshakable in her faith. She and Madonna House remained in the Church a veritable mountain of true faith. She was not impressed by the new scholarship; she did not need it to strengthen her faith. From her mother's womb she had been rooted in the Scriptures. The Gospels had been explained and lived in her family. She was deeply rooted in the Fathers, especially the Fathers of the Desert. Her faith had been severely tested in the fire, not seven times, but seventy times seven. With her faith remained her loyalty to the Holy Father, and her deep devotion to Mary, especially as Our Lady of Combermere. She was ready for anything!

All through the years Catherine had been considered by many as a radical, living on the fringe of Catholicism. She had been a sign of contradiction. Some said her work was from God; others said it was from the devil. But, depending totally upon God, Catherine had stood firmly for thirty years for what she had believed, often without any definite ecclesiastical approval. This was to change with the coming of Our Lady of Combermere.

Bishop William Smith of Pembroke came to Madonna House for the blessing and erection of the statue.[1] He brought the official recognition and approval of Madonna House Apostolate as a spiritual family in the Church. This approval showed clearly that Catherine was recognized as an obedient daughter of the Church, and her spiritual family was truly an authentic and official part of that Church. Catherine could hardly believe it was true!

With the blessing of the statue of Our Lady of Combermere, and the official approval of the Church for Madonna House, a new era began for Catherine. Now she was protected, no longer by God alone, but also by the whole Church in the person of her bishop. Had this approval not come at this time, who knows if the rebellious ones might have simply considered her a pioneer in the rebellious movement of the '60s? But now she was officially recognized as being truly Catholic, as being consistently faithful, and a true pillar of faith.

In all of this time of turmoil, from the '60s on, people would look to Catherine and to Madonna House for guidance much more than they had done previously. Throngs would come. Thousands would read her books. They would be published all over the world. They would be devoured by people searching for the true faith, for direction and discernment. Thanks be to God, it must be said that Catherine and Madonna House were faithful to their call, serving the Church unflinchingly in the terrible needs of the time.

---

1. June 8, 1960.

Before June 8, 1960, Catherine had been suspect in and out of the Church. Now she so grew in stature that all could behold one of the most faithful, loyal, wise and obedient daughters of the Church.

God chooses founders and foundresses to reveal to them the needs of his children — of his Church. He gives them an extraordinary discernment. They are like fathers and mothers to the world. They see clearly the changing needs of people, and move with these changes. They give their total selves to the satisfying of these needs.

With the opening of Vatican II, Catherine saw clearly that Catholics, wanting to be relevant, were becoming social activists. They were going to the inner city to engage in active work. The lacuna which developed in the '60s was in the realm of prayer. Priests, nuns, and laity began to pray less and less and to consider activity more important than prayer. Catherine had seen this coming. She, who had been a great pioneer of social action, saw that the pioneering which God now wanted of her was in the realm of prayer.

On the opening day of Vatican II, October 11, 1962, the first poustinia at Madonna House was blessed. Catherine's new work had begun. She would write more and more about the necessity of prayer. From now on she would establish prayer houses in various dioceses. Her book *Poustinia* would soon be born, and poustinias would arise all over the world.

In 1980 we received many letters from Bishops of Spanish-speaking countries in Latin America to whom Catherine had sent *Poustinia* translated into Spanish. Many responded, and they said astounding things, like: ''This book will help to re-christianize the Spanish-speaking people.'' The Bishop of San Salvador, who had succeeded Archbishop Romero, answered: ''Your book is helping me in my witness to face the problems that I have to face." He wrote a second time: "Thank you for your solidarity, for being with me at this time."

The influence of Madonna House, at present, is international, and this influence is due to two things: that Catherine has written many books under the inspiration of the Holy Spirit, which are being diffused all over the world; and, secondly, that through these books people come to realize that there is a living community (of Madonna House) which is attempting to live out these ideas. In other words, both the books and the living family of Madonna House, as twins in tandem — as one single cry — are proclaiming the Gospel of Jesus Christ and participating in the evangelization of the world at this time.

We are coming into a certain maturity as a family. We are beginning to understand better who we are. By the grace of God we have achieved a certain "sobornost," unity. Christ is present in Madonna House, which is a creation of the Father, Son, and Holy Spirit through the heart and hands and mind of the Mother of God, Our Lady of Combermere. Madonna House is a creation of God, far greater than anything we are able to conceive or imagine.

You cannot know people unless you love them. You cannot know a community created by God unless you love it. If we love it we will be loyal to its true spirit, and we will not allow any nefarious (or even holy) outside influences to change it from its authentic nature.

Through Catherine's vision God is inviting us to establish here a complete life where everything that is truly human and Christian will have a place. In other words, Madonna House is a city of God upon earth, a Christian civilization, a place where the human and the Christian blend, where Christ is incarnated in the human. Madonna House is meant to develop a very full and rich life, not only including work necessary for human existence, but also poetry, music, dancing, drama, the arts and handicrafts, helping the poor, hospitality, prayer — in short, the whole vision of Christian life which Catherine had been taught by God throughout her long and extraordinary life.

Chapter Seventeen

THE PINK HOUSE

As I have mentioned in several places, this book is not exactly a biography. I have recounted especially the events of Katia's early years to reflect on her life and character *as a whole,* often, in doing so, combining events which span many years. God willing, I hope in the future to continue a more detailed account of her life through the sixties and seventies. Lest the present volume become too long, I wish now to mention, before recounting her death, a series of incidents which to me were of great significance during the later Combermere period.

One day, in October, 1976, Catherine told me she had had a dream the previous night. "My mother came and told me that God still had lots of things for me to do, but not the ones I had in mind. God wants me to write! How do you like that!"

The following day I sat quietly near her while she slept. For the first time ever I saw something new on her face. Was it the shadow of death? Yet, I did not believe she had entered into her last illness. "Oh God, fill this void of loneliness, this immense hole at the core of her being, that she may live. Is it that we do not love her enough, or that our love cannot penetrate into her, or that you, jealous Lover, have placed a wall around her, your own encircling arms, which no one can enter? You live in her enclosed garden. She lives hidden in you, where no one of us can really reach her. Console her. Fill my heart with your peace, your love for her. Let me be present, simply present, to your work of love in her.''

On November 1 she called me over to her cabin. She was in great distress over her health. Her doctor was convinced that she suffered from severe heart trouble and could die any time from heart failure. He advised her to resign as Director General and rest more, act simply as a wise woman — a staretza — for the rest of the family. When she asked Fr. Callahan, her spiritual director, about it, he did not agree with resignation but wanted her to remain as Director of the women, and overall Director of the Apostolate, as long as she felt in her heart that God wanted her to do so.

The doctor's opinion was that Catherine pushed herself to exhaustion. Well, she had always lived like that, and God had always come through. Miracles have happened over and over again. She had always practiced what she preached to us — not to pay too much attention to your anxieties. Since we are so beloved by God and protected by him, he will save us from misery. To become anxious about tomorrow, or next week, poisons the present moment where God is intimately close in one's heart — available, loving, ready to heal, to give courage and direction for this moment.

Because of her heart condition, her internal struggle over her place in the Apostolate, and several other conflicts in the community, the year's end saw her swimming in an ocean of pain. She felt that 1977 was going to be a year of purification, and she had a need to get away for some thinking and praying. That's when she decided to go to the ''pink house.'' (The pink house is near our Casa de Nuestra Señora mission house in Winslow, Arizona. The outside is painted pink, and it was, through the generosity of a benefactor, made available to members of our community for rest and relaxation.)

En route we stopped off at the Mayo clinic in Rochester, MN, so Catherine could have a thorough medical check-up. The doctor told her that she had a slight heart-flutter and suffered from hyper-ventilation due to anxiety. At the end of the testing he pronounced her out of danger, and prescribed some medicine. He wanted her to rest more. Catherine prayed as follows: "Beloved Lord, Master of all and Servant of all, I pray to you in deep gratitude for my heart. I was ready to die, but you did not choose to take my life. But there are deaths and deaths. One is human death. The other is death to self which we all have to worry about. All of us are attached to unimportant things. If I knew I was dying, how many attachments would I have? All would vanish and you alone would shine. The monks of old prayed in a coffin once a month. It taught them detachment. Life is utterly useless unless lived in you. All of us have dreams of being good servants. But then in between we erect idols. We think we can slay them but we cannot. Our attachments are powerful. We ask total detachment and we are grateful. Teach us to be grateful so as to be totally detached and totally attached to you."

We arrived at the pink house January 22, and Catherine mused about her life and journey: "This is a pilgrimage we are on. My life, my youth, was filled with ideas of prayer and pilgrimage. As I grew up my pilgrimage became interiorized. I always wanted to go up the mountain of the Lord, but it all became a journey inward. Pilgrimage is the footprints of Christ and his footprints are all over the world. It is no longer a mountain but walking in the footsteps of Christ.''

''As if lightning struck, you begin to understand that life is not only a journey inward but also a journey outward. They are twins. You enter into a vortex, but not a turbulent vortex. It grabs you and, at times, you lose sense that you are following the footsteps of Christ. You begin to understand that you are following the whole Christ. It makes you dizzy.''

In a few weeks time, due to the rest, walking in the desert, lying in the sun, and (I thank God) the care I was able to give her, she began to recuperate. She said to me: ''I rest in your concern, your friendship. I can go to sleep at night peacefully, knowing that someone is within calling distance.'' ''My wounds are healing, she said, and I am slowly returning to the happiness I knew in the first fifteen years of my life. I am beginning to live again.''

Catherine had been put on a strict diet. In the course of her stay at the pink house she would lose twenty pounds.

But more important than the loss of physical weight during this time was the fact that she was able to speak about some of her heavy burdens. These conversations lifted thousands of pounds *off her heart*. One such burden concerned the Church.

On Sunday, February 13, she said, ''The whole Church is under attack by the devil. We Christians are too comfortable and hypnotized by the devil in so many ways.''

Two weeks later the dream she had had about her mother began to take on flesh. She was to enter now, after this period of recuperation, into a time of extraordinary literary output. (This is one of the reasons I chose to mention the pink house sojourn.) It was as if a period of crisis, through the grace of God, flowered into a period of new energy and inspiration.

Father Callahan had asked her some time ago to write about "sobornost," the Russian word for "unity." In a period of one month, from March 1 to April 4 Catherine wrote her book *Sobornost.* One month later, she was to begin her autobiography, *Fragments of My Life.* In July she would begin *Strannik,* (thus completing, with *Poustinia and Sobornost,* what she considered a kind of trilogy), and in August *Dear Father.* This was an amazingly inspired literary output in so short a time!

But not only did she channel this new energy into writing: she decided to go on a visitation of our mission houses! In May she was in Oregon, the Yukon, and Edmonton, Alberta; in June in Regina and Gravelbourg, Saskatchewan, Cleveland, Ohio, Ottawa. She returned to Combermere on July 3.

At the pink house she had said, "For the first time in fifty years I am able to rest, to really relax. I have gotten over my hurts because I was not alone. I had someone with whom to share the cross and the pain." I cannot thank God enough that he used me for these restorative months in her life. Her amazing strength, of course, came from God. She often said that she rested on God's heart and that her strength came from the cross.

These months with her were my own most important training days by the Lord. I see that now. Catherine was *my friend* there as well. No one understood me as she did. I am a priest with serious temptations, strong fears of rejection, but mingled with an immense attraction to God and a desire to do his will above all else. Those months at the pink house were also my own days of purification, formation, and renewal.

During these years also, she was invited to lecture to those involved in the charismatic renewal in America. She praised them for their prayer and encouraged them to keep moving into the heart of the Church. She reminded them of the importance of devotion to Mary, and asked them to always have a care for the poor.

She received several awards and honorary doctorates from universities and colleges; each presentation gave her an opportunity to proclaim the Gospel and call people to love Love.

March and April of 1981 found her in Europe, lecturing in Russian over Vatican Radio. She atttended Mass celebrated by Pope John Paul II in his private chapel.

In France, during a grace-filled two weeks, she attracted many of the spiritually hungry, lecturing to packed audiences. She had a deep encounter with her spiritual brother and son, Jean-Marie Lustiger, Archbishop of Paris. There were TV, radio, and newspaper interviews as well.

In England she lectured and was consulted by many. During Holy Week the BBC broadcast excerpts from her book *Poustinia*. Though she was now in her eighties these were rich, fruitful, apostolic years. Not bad for a young lady!

Chapter Eighteen

NOVGOROD, AND KATIA'S BROTHER ANDREW

Catherine had her own unique, Russian way of speaking about Madonna House, this community that God had created.

One day in June, 1984, she said to me:

I have understood why he brought me to America and why he created Madonna House. The Tartars had invaded the land in the 13th century, but they could never touch Novgorod. Novgorod continued to develop a very deeply Christian life. You have no idea how many geniuses and saints came out of Novgorod. Madonna House is a Novgorod. We are here to create a very rich human and Christian life, and we are like an island in the midst of a pagan, dehumanized world, just like Novgorod was a Christian island in the midst of a Tartar world. Novgorod was protected by the trees, by the forest of our faith, of our hope, of our love, so that they didn't really bother to penetrate it. And so we have to make sure that our 'forest' grows thicker and thicker — the forest of our faith, of our hope, of our love, so that the enemy can never penetrate here and destroy us.

And I said, "I think we are also Grad Kitisch." And she said, "Yes, yes, we are Grad Kitisch! Madonna

House is going to be a new Grad Kitisch. It will be like an island, a place where people can become human again, where the advance of so many inhuman things is going to be stopped either by God or by ourselves. Madonna House is going to be a refuge against the dehumanization of mankind.''

The Russians have always believed, as a legend, that at one time there existed a city — Grad (which means ''city'') Kitisch — which was totally Christian, and which one day was submerged in the waters of Lake Ladoga, just north of Leningrad. Some day this city, in God's good time, will rise up again from the waters and shine resplendent before the whole world.

Madonna House is to Catherine a Novgorod, which means a Christian civilization, as Christian as it can possibly be, free of materialism and any other un-Christian elements. It contains, in itself, the seeds for Christian cultures of the future.

On another day, in December of the same year, Catherine called me on the phone in my little room at Madonna House. She was very excited. She said:

> I've discovered more about who I am, about what God is doing at Madonna House. What is the heart of my kind of poverty? I used to think it was physical poverty, the poverty of those who are hungry, who are in need of food, clothing and shelter. And that's true. That still is true. I am immensely concerned about that. I've always been concerned about the poverty of those who don't have food, who are hungry, who need clothes, who are suffering from physical needs.
>
> But I have discovered tonight — as my mind was pacing up and down — I felt something was in the making. My mind, my heart, were on the edge of a revelation, and I was all excited. All of a sudden it came to me: the real poverty in this world is the poverty of those who have no faith, of those who do not believe in God. So few people indeed believe in God. I thought

of the writings and novels of Dostoyevsky where he speaks about the same kind of thing.

And so I discovered that the poverty which my heart seeks to alleviate, the poor that my whole heart wants to enrich, to touch, are those who have no faith. That is why God has put into my heart the desire to write and write and write, so that people may come to believe in him, so that people may come to love him. That is another great discovery for me. After Madonna House being Novgorod, being Grad Kitisch, now, thank God, this is another one.

The poverty Madonna House is meant to alleviate, the hunger to be fed, concerns those whose spirits linger in a terrible weakness, those who are spiritually famished, spiritually starved, spiritually anaemic. Madonna House is meant to feed that poverty, to help people to come to a knowledge of God and to love him. Madonna House is to bolster the faith of many and to bring to thousands and millions the message of God's love. Our apostolate is to every person and to every need, but at this time especially to those who are spiritually starved, spiritually poor, to those who have no faith and who do not love God.

She was totally delighted and excited about this discovery, and she added: "I wanted to share it with you right away, right away." And I said: "I am delighted too. I am so happy to hear of this wonderful discovery, because it is absolutely true and it gives a clearer direction for our lives, our prayer, our fasting, our activities, at this time of our history."

In a recent major theological work, Catherine's spirituality was described as "another individually orientated spirituality, but with a Russian flavoring." If by "individual" one means an absolute emphasis on the radical change of one's own heart as the basis for change in society, then, yes, Catherine lays absolute priority on that interior, individual revolution.

But her doctrine, far from being limited to seeking out one's own personal perfection, far from being individually orientated, is very broad, seeking the fulness of truth, and involved in an all-comprehensive love for God and everyone and everything. Her doctrine, in all her works, is directed both to loving God and loving others by practical service, by prayer, by adoration, and, of course, by taking care of the needs of the poor.

All her life she has been in the vanguard of social justice, as well as the prayer movement. In the thirties, social justice was absent from the Church. Therefore, God inspired her to dedicate the best of her efforts to social justice. Gradually, other people caught on fire. The social encyclicals finally became known.

In the sixties, hundreds, thousands of nuns, priests, and laity discovered the inner city, the poor, and gave their lives to them. But then another lacuna appeared in the Church: prayer was being downgraded. Again, God moved in the heart of his servant Catherine and inspired her to remedy this situation, to heal this wound. It was then she began to write extensively on prayer. It was then she was moved to establish the first poustinia at Madonna House and to begin speaking about discovering God in one's own heart. She, who for many years had stressed discovering God in other people, especially in the poor, now was led by God to speak about his presence in one's own heart, in the "poustinia of the heart." Listen to her own response:

> World reform is easy. Madonna House stands for self-reform. The betterment of the world starts with me. When I am converted, renewed, less selfish, then the whole Church, the whole world, is changed for the better.

> My answer to atheism, to indifference, is a community which lives in such a way that it proclaims by its

very existence that God exists... a community of the poor, of the anawim, who depend on God for everything and who love each other.

To the loneliness produced by depersonalization, by technology, computers, electronic communication, I answer by a person-to-person apostolate. That is why we have listening houses. Social action to help the poor, the needy, will always be necessary. I want it on a person-to-person basis most of the time.

Madonna House speaks a resounding 'No' to all nuclear weapons, to weapons of any kind. We are opposed to women priests. We meet children here at Madonna House all the time and we *know* how much children these days are in *need of their mothers.* Madonna House responds basically to the peace movement, to social justice, to the many problems facing mankind today, by each person loving God, loving each other, doing the duty of the moment with great love, and offering to others the hospitality of the heart as well as of the home.

I have mentioned earlier that Catherine at the present time has one living sibling, her youngest brother Andrew. As this chapter concerns Catherine's reflections on how Madonna House reminded her of the ideals of Holy Russia, I thought it would be the appropriate place to tell you about Andrew's visit to Combermere. During his visit he too saw how Madonna House reflected his Russian ideals.

One day in the early months of 1982 Catherine received a letter from Andrew who lives in Cuba. He announced that he would be visiting Madonna House sometime in June, July, or August. Catherine was utterly delighted! It had been more than thirty years — 1939 — since they had seen each other.

He arrived on a Sunday, July 4, 1982. I met him in

the yard and immediately we walked over to St. Kate's where Catherine had been eagerly expecting him for the last few hours. She was sitting in bed, looking very lovely, radiant.

He walked up to her. They embraced, they cried, they immediately began speaking in Russian. He sat down, got up again, embraced her again, sat down, embraced her again several times. They visited for about half an hour. Then we walked back over the bridge.

Before going into the main house he said, ''Let's wait a while. I don't want anybody to see me crying.'' Finally we walked in. He shook hands with everyone and sat down with several of the family for a bit of supper. He reluctantly ate the beef, lettuce, strawberries and cream that had been prepared for him.

He spoke right away about Madonna House: ''I like this place. It is a fantastic group of people. They don't live for themselves; they live for others. If we want to live an interesting, exciting life we have to live for others. My sister has done something beautiful here. She herself is a wonderful person, I can see that already.''

He was disappointed that he was not staying in one of the dorms: ''I want to take part in this family. Don't put me aside all by myself.'' Andrew speaks Russian, Spanish, English, but French, he said, was his best language. He is approximately 5'8'', in his late sixties, of robust health, and gives the impression of unusual moral strength. He is internationally famous as a judo expert. He spoke neither of Marxism nor capitalism but of a social justice based on the Gospel.

On the following day, Andrew was given a tour of Madonna House. He was most interested in everything he saw. He was quite moved and awed by the friendship, community, love and understanding that exists in Madonna House. He wondered if we had been concerned about his political views. He is deeply committed to Cuba, to Judo, to physical education, and to the poor. He loves the Church and rejoices that now it is no longer aligned with the rich.

Concerning Madonna House he said: "Here, true Christianity is being lived. Once this kind of life is known, it should spread all over the world. I truly believe this is the Church of the future."

He refuses to eat much meat because his friends and associates in Cuba seldom see meat. He has the old-world gentlemanly manner, a deep sense of his own dignity and the dignity of others. As he spoke with his sister for an hour or so, expressing his doubts, his questions, his concerns, he said to me, as he was about to leave, "Will you allow me one favor?" I said, "Certainly." He said, "I would like to embrace you for all the care you are giving my sister." He took me in his strong (Russian!) arms, embraced me heartily, and there were tears in his eyes.

Andrew, as a highly esteemed teacher at the University of Havana, is giving his life for the formation of young people. He teaches character training, self-discipline, motivation, service, love, acceptance of others, dedication. He himself believes in God. At Mass he said: "I felt the presence of a superior Being. God is present in this chapel."

He was terribly moved by people coming to give him the kiss of peace. "Madonna House is built on love and faith," he said. Incredible as it sounds, he actually exclaimed: "Here I find humanity at its highest level. I see that the Church has changed. It now desires to be at the service of the human race. The human Church has been a terrible burden upon my heart, but now I have hope. We understand each other; we can communicate."

Every time he came near Catherine he wept quietly, hiddenly. He was so delighted to finally be with her. He had tried to come on previous occasions but without success. So he had quite an experience with us. On another occasion he said: "Madonna House is first of all God, then Catherine, then the community; everything is penetrated by God and dedicated to the service of others. This is the way to live." He was awed by the quality of Christian culture he found at Madonna House, that is, how the values of the Gospel penetrated and influenced every aspect of life.

The secretary of the Communist Party at the University is an ex-pupil of his and a very dear friend, "The most noble man I have ever met," Andrew said. "When I return I will speak to him most magnificently about everything I have seen here at Madonne House."

Andrew stayed with us for several weeks. On his last day a special supper table was set for him, Catherine and me in her cabin. We sat down to a fine Russian meal of rice bouillon, cabbage, delicious Russian cutlets, coffee and ice cream. Catherine had prepared the menu.

During the course of the table conversation Andrew exclaimed: "My mother was a real saint, a real saint! These piroshky remind me of her. And the Russian cutlets! I haven't had any in years, in years. This is just like home!"

Catherine said: "My mother taught me everything." Reminiscing, Andrew spoke about his father's death. "I was ten years old. We were in Finland. That day he had been unwell. He had sent me to the pharmacy for some medicine. When I returned, he was dead."

Andrew said: "My sister and I are very close. We are both working for the same thing. We both want a better world. Her books have a great influence.

Madonna House is a wonderful community. Here people can really develop.''

Around 7 p.m. they embraced, knowing departure was near. They spoke in Russian. Catherine wept. She was grey as he broke away from her. To me he whispered in Spanish, ''come with me.'' Outside, he let loose his grief. ''I love her so much. I do not weep, I do not weep. I have to be strong.'' We walked around for a few minutes until he recovered himself. Just before we finally parted he put his hands on my shoulders and gave me a solemn commission: ''As the oldest member of the Kolyschkine family, I entrust my sister to you.'' And he walked away.

Andrew has been back several times, and we hope he can soon return again. As Catherine's brother you can imagine what a special place he has in all our hearts. We call him ''Uncle Andrew'' and we love him more than words can tell.

Chapter Nineteen

KATIA'S DEATH

Beginning in 1981, Catherine entered upon what we call her great illness, which was to culminate in her death. During it, she almost died several times. I cannot go into those extraordinary years in any great detail here, but I want to witness to the fact that they were years when, through her illness, many, many hurts and wounds of the family were healed — among ourselves, each person with Catherine and she with each one, and with people who had left the apostolate. During the last couple of years we used to take turns sitting with her, being with her, chatting, or just praying in silence while she slept or dozed. During those hours many, many healings took place among us; we can all testify to that. It was obvious that she was offering her life for the "sobornost" she saw as the goal of this family of Madonna House which God had created.

During Catherine's last great illness I constantly prayed for three things: first, that she might do the will of God perfectly right up to the very end; second, (as we pray in the Eastern liturgy,) "that the end of her life may be Christian, painless, unashamed and peaceful, and for a good defense before the awesome judgment seat of Christ''; third, that God would give me the grace of being present during her final moments on earth. All these prayers were answered beyond my greatest expectations.

Let me recount some of the events of the days leading up to her death.

We were all convinced that under any other circumstances, and even in the best of hospitals, Catherine would not have survived as long as she did. The only place she could possibly have survived is in her cabin, St. Kate's. The reason for this is that, besides the care, the food, etc., what really kept her alive was the love of her family. God used her in a powerful way to teach all of us how to look after the chronically ill.

The community looked after her with such tenderness and love and gentleness, like looking after a little child who could fail to thrive through lack of love. This love was the main ingredient in Catherine's on-going care. The mystery we had to face is why her life was prolonged in this painful way. My own answer was that her presence was of immense importance to the Apostolate, the Church, and to the entire world. In some special way, God blessed all of our lives; and in some mysterious way, touched the whole earth with her continuing presence.

At 5:15, on the morning of Saturday, December 14, 1985, the Feast of St. John of the Cross, the buzzer rang in my little poustinia, calling me urgently to her side. I knew instinctively it was the end. I ran over, not even noticing the bitter cold, realizing that she was about to breathe her soul to God. I gave her a final absolution for all of her sins, placed a particle of the Consecrated Host upon her tongue, took her in my arms, and prayed, ''Jesus, Mary and Joseph. Jesus, Mary and Joseph.''

She did not open her eyes, but she recognized my

voice and listened carefully as I said, ''Mother Mary, thank you for Katia. Katia, we love you and we thank you for everything.''

She relaxed completely, and fell asleep in the Lord like a little girl, full of trust and contentment. It was 5:28 A.M. The family had been alerted, and as each came in he or she kissed Catherine with joy and great reverence; especially her son, George.

Catherine lived at the heart of the Church and of history. She had been dynamically related — through concern and understanding — to the major events of this century. To be associated with her was to have lived a very exciting life: laying down one's life for others, being a light and a hope to many during this period of intense darkness and incredible disarray. By being associated with Catherine you did not view the dramas of our times from afar, or as a spectator, but rather, being united with her, you found yourself playing a substantial role.

She was a rich human being. If religion is a relationship, and life is wholeness, if wisdom is being in harmony with all that exists, then she was a most holy human being. I knew of few, if any, men or women, who are, or were, better related to the triune God, to Jesus, Mary, the angels, the saints. From buttons to the cosmos, she was related to everything in a personal way.

At home in all cultures, she never ceased to react to all things according to her own proper formation. She had given many people a love for, and an understanding of, Russia and Russian Orthodoxy, and Eastern spirituality. She loved as God loves, without reservations, in total acceptance, bearing the other's inadequacies, forgiving sins, and always strengthening people. She had been a friend, a sister, a mother to many. It was an immense gift of God to have been able to share a life such as hers, one of the greatest lives ever lived; to have been drawn, through association with her, into such intimacy with God, people, and the universe.

Because of her and Father Callahan, and Eddie Doherty, God had revealed himself to hundreds of people at Madonna House, and to thousands all over the world; through them, he had revealed himself to me. He now draws us all to himself in a powerful and moving way, putting into our hearts a passionate love for him. That, of course, is the greatest gift we received from Catherine and Father Callahan, a gift so immense it will take one's whole life — eternity — to appreciate.

Because of God, Jesus and Mary, everything takes on meaning, beauty, purpose, holiness. Since my association with Katia I have not had a single boring day! Catherine has brought me into the very heart of God. How often she had spoken deep and consoling words which answered the questions in my heart even before I knew how to formulate them — even before I *knew what they were!* Daily, she shed light on my darkness. Her spiritual readings and talks healed, disturbed, strengthened and consoled.

It was fun to be with her! Her sense of humor rarely failed. Her basic lightness of heart, her peace, her love, her childlike wonder, her wide and deep interests, her passionate love for God and for others, her radiance when she talked about Jesus — all this made her a most fascinating and intriguing person!

God led her across many countries, physically and symbolically, down deep valleys and up high mountains, through cyclones, hurricanes, tempests, on land and sea, through darkness, thunder and lightnings. Yet, in her depths, she inhabited a vast, radiant, expansive, peaceful land where the sun shines all day.

She had known the deepest depths and the highest

mountains, the summits and the pits of human existence. She had been involved with God — Father, Son and Holy Spirit — with Our Lady, the angels, the saints, people on earth, and the enemy who had made every effort to cripple her, to tempt her, to kill her, to destroy her in some way or another.

The future holds even more difficulties, more possible tragedies, for the human race. Catherine remained alert, aware, but peaceful, fully present to God in the moment, leaving the past to his mercy and interceding for the future. She continued to experience rejections, loneliness, agony. To her, all that was normal, her ordinary state and vocation. She had no self-pity, not a whimper.

One day in July, 1976, I was on retreat in Carriacou, in the West Indies. God gave me a vision of her pain, and invited me to be a Simon of Cyrene to her Cross, to be to her a brother and a friend.

I was meditating on Catherine — her person, her place in the Church, her relationship with God. I wrote the following in my diary:

'' 'Two things are great,' says the northeast Brazilian fisherman, 'God and the sea.' As I sit in the golden sunshine watching the blue-green Caribbean topped by whiteness, I think to myself, 'Two persons are great, God and Catherine!' She carries within herself a special presence of God and shares him with everyone she meets. She speaks the word of God clearly and illuminates each event, each circumstance, each problem, with a wise and holy word of God. God reveals himself through her as awesome, humble, wise, tender and infinitely merciful, whether she is sorting buttons or assisting at the liturgy.

She is a genius, a passionate woman, and a prophet. As a prophet, she is constantly given a vision of the world and of people as God sees it. As a prophet, she is compelled to shout the truth to the whole world, to pass on what she hears from God. So often she has been tormented with pressure from God to speak; how often have I heard her say: 'I *have* to speak. I can't help it. I don't want to but I have to.'

The vision she sees is so all-absorbing, so exciting, and at times so frightful, that she bypasses the 'niceties' every now and then. She is a woman in a hurry to speak passionately of the inspirations passed on to her by her passionate Lover. Her voice, strong and plangent, sounds forth across Madonna House and the world. This voice — constantly, daily, little by little — forms this community, prods the conscience of the whole Church, dynamically influences the lives of many. Truly we are a 'word of God' community.

What does she experience? The cross. She remains on the cross where her Lover is crucified — Christ in agony in each person until the end of time.

Loneliness. Like Dorothy Day's, Catherine's also is a 'long loneliness,' this year perhaps more so than in the last few years, due to Eddie's death, my illness, the loss of some of her closest associates. But now, more of her own family share her vision and desire to lay down their lives for each other and for the Church. She will become aware of this tremendous growth in a year or two. At present, she is still caught up in the 'loss,' and sustaining the Apostolate more or less single-handedly.

Crucified, she longs for the company of other crucified people. Her great frustration always comes from her seeming inability to bring people to the fulness of truth and love, to a passionate love of her Lover, the Lord Jesus Christ. Often she says: 'I am letting God down. He loves us so much. We must love him wholeheartedly in return.'

Hence, she is as single-minded as a bulldozer, untiring as a tornado, relentless as the ocean waves beating at our shores, passionate as a tigress. These gigantic gifts have enabled her to survive; any kind of compromise with pettiness would have destroyed her. Madonna House was born and brought to a high degree of spiritual maturity through her. The Church has been vastly influenced by her message from God, not only through her writings but through the community which incarnates her teachings.''

It seemed to me that these were some of the deepest insights about Catherine I ever received, and that they would serve as a fitting conclusion to this little book. She was a passionate woman in love with God. I am convinced that her spiritual legacy will be a life-giving stream in the Church for all centuries to come.

How do I relate to a crucified person? By allowing myself to be crucified near her. To a prophet? By welcoming her in the inn of my heart. How do I live with a bulldozer? By standing on the side and letting her freely do her job. How do I live with a whirlwind? By not expecting her always to be a gentle breeze (most of the time she *is* a gentle breeze). How do I associate with a tigress? By loving her cub, the Apostolate. How do I respond to a holy, passionate woman? By cherishing her love for me, by accepting it — for truly it is divine!

My greatest conflict with Catherine has been the inability to discern — when someone gets hurt — whether the words spoken are the truth of God, or whether they come from her own weakness. The solution to this dilemma is simply to express it when it happens. If the words come from her humanness, she will admit it. A prophet has an immense need to be heard. I pray God to make of me a good listener, to be a bridge between her words and other people when they misunderstand each other, to be a friend who constantly stands at her side, encouraging, consoling one who suffers so much and has been entrusted by God with such a shattering mission.

When the words God places in her heart and mind are rejected, she suffers doubly — first, that God is being rejected; secondly, from the continual rubbing of her own immense wound of rejection. I must help her to be healed of the terrible pain of rejection by understanding, friendship and fidelity.

She desires passionately to pass on to her own spiritual family the encyclopedic knowledge she possesses in so many areas. She has indeed been well trained by her parents, and loves to teach, to pass it on. She is a born lecturer, but she prefers small groups, her own staff sitting around her, learning from her.

Her father trained her to be the best at everything. He demanded much from her. She loved him. She tried, therefore, to respond to his directives. She knew they came from love.

I am on retreat these months in Carriacou to be renewed in the spirit so I can better care for, love, support and serve Catherine, in God's good time. My own love affair with God moves forward, and I want to surrender my whole self to him, to do his will, to love him passionately — this is the ideal of my life.

The prophet, the visionary, climbs the mountain alone, like Jesus who went out onto the mountain to pray alone. But a friend can accompany the prophet and enter into a similar silence and solitude, making the loneliness bearable, changing it even into companionship.''[1]

To have been the friend of such a prophet — to have helped in some way to make her loneliness more bear-

---

1. Meditation, Carriacou, 1976.

able — this has been the greatest gift of my life. In this book, I have tried to share something of what this gift has meant to me.

AFTERWARD

Catherine was a joy to my heart. She was childlike, like a little girl. She was always determined to become better, but not in a harsh, aggressive way; rather in a simple, humble effort. Her kindness to me was infinite, like God's. It was a balm upon my soul, and undoubtedly a great means which the Lord Jesus ordained for my personal salvation.

When I was ordained a priest I loved the priesthood above everything else in this world. But I had not yet determined to become a saint. I just wanted to love people very simply.

That's what I tried to do all my life. And God has blessed me infinitely. No matter what may happen to me in the future, I have already been blessed. For I found in Catherine's love for me the utter purity, wholeness, and infinity of God's love.

I can look up to God now, and to Our Lady, and say in all sincerity, ''Thank you for her love.''

To have had in your life *one person* who understood you, who loved you totally — that is more than enough for one life. For such a relationship is an explosion of joy, of God's life into your life. I can never thank God enough for the love of Catherine de Hueck Doherty for me. *Like many others who knew her,* I have been the recipient of a great love.

Imprimerie des Éditions Paulines
250, boul. St-François Nord
Sherbrooke, QC, J1E 2B9

Imprimé au Canada — Printed in Canada